The Unholy Bible

Hebrew Literature from the Time of David to the Beginnings of Greek Influence

NEW AUTONOMY SERIES
Jim Fleming & Peter Lamborn Wilson, Editors

TAZ
THE TEMPORARY AUTONOMOUS
ZONE, ONTOLOGICAL ANARCHY,
POETIC TERRORISM
Hakim Bey

THIS IS YOUR FINAL WARNING!
Thom Metzger

FRIENDLY FIRE
Bob Black

CALIBAN AND THE WITCHES
Silvia Federici

INVISIBLE GOVERNANCE
THE ART OF AFRICAN MICROPOLITICS
David Hecht & Maliqalim Simone

WARCRAFT
Jonathan Leake

THIS WORLD WE MUST LEAVE
Jacques Camatte

THE ELECTRONIC DISTURBANCE
Critical Art Ensemble

SPECTACULAR TIMES
Larry Law

FUTURE PRIMITIVE
John Zerzan

WHORE CARNIVAL
Shannon Bell

X-TEXTS
Derek Pell

CRACKING THE MOVEMENT
SQUATTING BEYOND THE MEDIA
Foundation for the Advancement
of Illegal Knowledge

THE LIZARD CLUB
Steve Abbott

FIRST AND LAST EMPERORS
THE ABSOLUTE STATE &
THE BODY OF THE DESPOT
Kenneth Dean & Brian Massumi

WIGGLING WISHBONE
STORIES OF PATASEXUAL SPECULATION
Bart Plantenga

CRIMES OF CULTURE
Richard Kostelanetz

PIRATE UTOPIAS
MOORISH CORSAIRS &
EUROPEAN RENEGADOES
Peter Lamborn Wilson

ELECTRONIC CIVIL DISOBEDIENCE
Critical Art Ensemble

THE UNHOLY BIBLE

HEBREW LITERATURE FROM THE TIME OF DAVID
TO THE BEGINNINGS OF GREEK INFLUENCE
(1000 – 300 BC)

*The "Secular" Literature of the Hebrew
Kingdom and Second Commonwealth,
Incorporated into the Bible and Whitewashed
into a Pious Appearance in all Available
Translations and Traditional Commentaries*

Jacob Rabinowitz

AUTONOMEDIA

Acknowledgements

The first order of thanks go to Leo Weinstock and Bob Fradkin: what Hebrew I have I owe to their excellent instruction, passion for language, and generosity with time.

I am also indebted to my friends at Step-by-Step Farm: Penny Novack, for our decade long argument on the nature of God, which she basically won; Michael Novack, for his encyclopaedic knowlege of the ancient world, and particularly his insights into the book of Job; and Beth Novack, the inspiration of my translation of the Song of Songs: once more I lay these verses adoringly at my *Layla*'s feet, with a whispered *ya habibi* from her distant *Majnun*.

Brett Rutherford of Grim Reaper Books brought out a very handsome chapbook version of the Song of Songs: I thank him once again for his deft assistance and re-admire his sense of the elegant.

Finally I thank Peter Lamborn Wilson, from whose excellent suggestions the work has taken on added clarity and luster.

Copyright © 1995 Autonomedia

Autonomedia
POB 568 Williamsburgh Station
Brooklyn, New York 11211-0568 USA

Phone & Fax: 718-963-2603

Printed in the United States of America

Contents

Preface 7

King Solomon's Book of Love Songs
        (*Song of Solomon*). 15

Selections from *The Book of Praises* (*Psalms*) 31

How? (*The Lamentations of Jeremiah*). 39

Job 55

Solomon's Testimony (*Ecclesiastes*) 127

Textual and Bibliographical Notes 152

Preface

I

In this volume you hold virtually the entire literary record of Kingdom-period Israel, an erotic, pagan, aristocratic, impious and elegant world, closer in spirit to Homer than to Hosea. This incredible record of vivid life was too central to the national identity to be jettisoned by the compilers of the Bible, so it was reinterpreted, muffled, even muzzled. Yet this literature, allowed to deliver its message directly, can tell us a great deal about the early Hebrew religious culture that produced it, the prophetic voices that were raised against it, and the Rabbinic religion that replaced it.

In a sense this is the "missing link" for our understanding of the Biblical world: we have been long taught to view the Jews as a nation of priests, prophet-led and pure, and have forgotten that they were a real people, the Hebrews, the ancient Israelis, a Bronze-age Middle-Eastern Kingdom as riotous and exotic as the court of Agamemnon.

II

The most important question that can be posed in regard to this volume is "how accurate is it?" Earlier translations have accepted the viewpoint of Rabbinic Judaism: it was this party who assembled, edited and sealed the Scriptures.

The Unholy Bible

The Christian reading is based on the Rabbinic, with of course the necessary departures on specific points. These interpretations were by religious scholars who based their decisions on the authority of Faith, and whose vision of religion was solemn. Even the Higher Criticism scholars of the 19th and 20th centuries show the profound influence of the religious interpretation — in rejection of readings which show a playful or "impious" spirit. The result of this 2,000-year interfaith agreement on the true sense of the Bible has been, where not simple censorship, a "scrambling" of any material that contradicts piety.

Take the most difficult of the texts, *Job*. The book makes perfect sense, and in fact is one of the best-preserved in the Bible. It requires *virtually no emendation*. (I note here that the *Anchor Bible* shifts twenty-line segments from one end of the book to the other, likewise the *New English Bible* freely shuffles whatever seems inconvenient; the *Jewish Publication Society's* editions, though unintelligible, at least keep intact what they can't understand.)

Though to expose the shortcomings of previous translations in detail would be an encyclopedic task, it is only fair to give the reader at least one parade example. For this, chapter 19 of *Job* will serve very well. Here we find Job appealing to God, against God, for justice. This implies that God has in fact been unjust. So unacceptable has this suggestion been to later piety that all translations have falsified the lines that manifest it. The lines are, literally:

24) Who will give (idiom for "would that" or "if only") then that my words were written, engraved forever in a book

25) with a pen of iron and lead (i.e., with a pen of iron on lead, like our "with pen and paper"), hewn forever into rock

26) so I would know that that which will vindicate me

8

Preface

exists and at the last will stand up on the dust (i.e., here on earth),

27) and after my hide is destroyed — this (sc. will survive), and without my flesh I will (sc. through this piece of writing) gaze at God

28) whom I wish to see for myself, with my own eyes, not another's.

The lines are difficult, but far from impossible. The *King James* version goes:

Oh that my words were now written! oh that they were printed in a book!

That they were graven with an iron pen and lead in the rock for ever!

For I know that my redeemer liveth, and that he shall stand at the latter day upon the earth:

And though after my skin worms destroy this body, yet in my flesh I shall see God:

whom I shall see for myself, and my eyes shall behold, and not another.

Here the sense has been clearly twisted to fit in with Christian eschatology — the word "redeemer" is what this reading hangs on: it is a misrendering of the Hebrew *goali* — which may mean variously who or whatever vindicates, defends or stands up for. The only antecedent for the term "vindicator" is the writing itself. To provide the pious image of "patient Job," Job is made to express confidence that God will "redeem" him. But if God is going to redeem him, why does Job want an *eternal record* of his complaint?

This reading has long since been abandoned by scholars as a wishful Christian re-write. The question is, what replaced it? The *New English Bible* has:

The Unholy Bible

O that my words might be inscribed,
O that they might be engraved in an inscription,
cut with an iron tool and filled with lead
to be a witness in hard rock!
But in my heart I know that my vindicator lives
and he will rise last to speak in court;
and I shall discern my witness standing at my side
and see my defending counsel, even God himself,
whom I shall see with my own eyes,
I myself and no other.

This is no more than a unitarian version of the *King James*
— the explicitly Christian material is muted, but the same
solution obtains. The *New English* version has invented three
lines and twisted the surrounding syntax to pass this off. The
reader may now judge for himself whether my rendering
doesn't better fit the text:

If only my words were written down, inscribed in the
pages of a book,
    writ with iron pen, cut into sheets of lead, hewn forever
into stone!
    I'd know I had a living witness, lasting past, standing up
for me on earth,
    so when this body wrecks and rots I could, with my words,
still stare back accusingly at God —
    if only I could confront him myself, with my own and
actual eyes!

This reading of the text requires no importations or inven-
tions: what it does ask is an understanding of Job's theological position: that Job is demanding justice from a God he
believes to be unjust. The purpose for the eternal inscription

Preface

of Job's charges against God now becomes clear. Job expects nothing better than death from his deity, but craves, as a final malign satisfaction, an ineffaceable reproach to confront God forever with how shabbily God has acted.

The concept of an unjust God, or a man more just than God, is intolerable to the pious mind, so the tragic desperation of Job's demand for Theodicy, and the inescapability of its paradoxic form, are candied over with inserted assertions that God will make all fine.

One could multiply examples of such tendentious mistranslation, and others that are just silly — censoring the penis off Behemoth, for example, though a giant tail on an animal modelled on the Hippo is improbable, and the word "testicles" — decorously translated "belly" — occurs in the same line. Or the venerable unintelligibility of "by the skin of my teeth" — the Hebrew actually reads "I escaped with nothing but the teeth in my head," (lit. "the teeth in my flesh," i.e., in my gums). Far from exciting disquiet, the meaningless phrase has been passed solemnly along: what does it mean? That only a layer of plaque stands between Job and disaster?

My own method of translation is neither free nor academic; rather it is what I like to call *historical*. Every nuance of meaning that would have been evident to the contemporary reader (or listener) has been brought forth with elaborate care, often by means of paraphrase or even anachronism. That is, all the information ordinarily given in footnotes is here presented as part of the text, to permit a coherent and fully informed reading immediately. This is notwithstanding a precise and accurate translation of the texts, interpreting and paraphrasing, but never inventing.

To give an impression of the kinds of change this entails, I will give an example of excellent, conscientious scholarly translation, and then show how mine differs. The best for

The Unholy Bible

sheer text is the Jewish Publication Society's *Tanakh* (1985) — praiseworthy for its traditional Jewish reluctance to alter the document in any way, preferring a difficult reading to the dubious clarity of an emendation. This means that obscurities of the text tend to remain obscure, but at least one can see what's *there*. The passage is from *The Book of Lamentations*, Chapter 4, verses 1–3:

> Alas!
> The gold is dulled,
> Debased the finest gold!
> The sacred gems are spilled
> At every street corner.
> The precious children of Zion;
> Once valued as gold —
> Alas, they are accounted as earthen pots,
> Work of a potter's hands!
> Even jackals offer the breast
> And suckle their young;
> But my poor people has turned cruel,
> Like ostriches in the desert.

My rendering is:

> Is it possible gold can tarnish, or silver lose its worth?
> precious stones left lying in the street?
> Yet Zion's golden children are thrown away like paper.
> The desert jackal will offer her teat and give the cub suck,
> but my people's women have lost even that brute and common tenderness,
> they're like the desert ostrich
> that lays and leaves its eggs on the ground to be crushed under every foot.

Preface

It must be borne in mind that we are dealing with a text that is 2,500 years old, half a millenium more ancient than Vergil and from a culture even more different from ours. Thus some of the conventions of rhetoric have to be changed to make a clear reading — for example, the Hebrew introduces the first lines as metaphor with the word "Alas!" whereas English requires the form of the "rhetorical question" to achieve the same sense.

In verse two the image of worthlessness is cheap pottery, the "throw-away" commodity of the ancient Near East, where *paper* was rare and valuable. For *us* paper occupies the same status (think of paper plates and napkins.)

In verse three the Hebrew expects the reader to know the folkloric valuation of the ostrich, which in English must be supplied.

Obviously the *Tanakh* rendering, or good scholarly ones such as one usually finds in the *Anchor Bible* are preferable for quotation in a learned essay which will advance new interpretations of the text. But I believe my method offers, without sacrificing accuracy, something just as important as scholarly ultra-precision. These books are *literature*, and have a level of meaning which reveals itself in terms of beauty, imagination, and power. A less free rendering than mine, stopping at what each individual word *means*, will fail to convey the way words, taken together, achieve the *meaningful*. Even if the proper sense is supplied in critical notes, the result cheats the reader — instead of a vision of a lost world, he gets exhausting mini-lessons in history and Hebrew.

1
King Solomon's Book of Love Songs

Commonly called the "Song of Songs" or the "Song of Solomon"

The verses here seem to be a collection of traditional, popular wedding and love songs — beyond that near certainty we enter the realm of conjecture. Modern scholars tend to think it contains datable material from the time of Solomon's accession (c. 960 BC) — the "Royal Epithalamion," 3:6–11 — to the period of Persian influence in the 6th and 5th centuries BC — the Persian word for garden, *pardes*, 4:13.

Setting aside, for the sake of conservatism, the high likelihood that some of the material was old even in Solomon's time, the book may cautiously be said to range from the 10th to the 5th centuries, which means that much of it antedates Homer by two or three hundred years, while a good portion was written by the contemporaries of Sappho and Anacreon, who write with a similar playful, erotic delicacy. The latest compositions were indited while Aristophanes still breathed.

It does not seem to me unreasonable to suppose that Solomon was responsible for the assembly of the book in its entirety. The use of the word *pardes* is as strong as the late-date

The Unholy Bible

evidence gets, which is not very. It is more than plausible that Solomon, who accomplished a program of cultural consolidation comparable to those of Augustus or Charlemagne, would have ordered the anthology made. The idea has behind it the momentum of tradition, the book's title, careful structure and graceful shifts and recapitulations of theme, all of which, by my reading, point to a single, brilliant compiler.

But, whether we allow ourselves to invest the songs with historic range or royal glamour — or both — our understanding is not affected. Nothing in the text emerges with added clarity for being fixed to a certain date.

Completely secular and sensuous, the book required vigorous defensive mystical interpretation before its Jewish scriptural status was decisively confirmed at the Council of Jamnia in 90 AD. The Christians, adopting the Bible, adapted the Talmudic reading of the songs as a love-dialogue between God and his chosen people, and the book radiated its influence, on two cultures, for the next 1800 years, through a mist of allegoric confusion. Two traditional Jewish readings will show variously the strength and weakness of the approach. The knocking of the lover in 5:2 (*King James Version*), "I sleep, but my heart waketh: it is the voice of my beloved that knocketh, saying, Open to me, my sister, my love, my dove, my undefiled..." The lover is held to be God calling to the soul even in sleep, pounding, insisting it wake and hear, and the knocking is the heartbeat itself — for the mere fact of existence, tokened by the rhythm of one's blood, summons like a drumbeat to remembrance of God.

One would gladly jettison higher criticism for a complete allegory of this order, but the poem itself rejects it, driving a pious explicator to heights of unfortunate ingenuity, as when, confronted by the breasts in 4:5, he primly interprets them as Moses and Aaron.

King Solomon's Book of Love Songs

It is worth reviewing the major later interpretations, as good modern translations, of which the best is the *New English Bible*, exhibit traces of both. In the 18th and 19th centuries it was the scholarly fashion to read our book as a play about Solomon, a shepherd girl and her rustic lover. In the early 20th the suggestion was made that the book contained cult-hymns from Canaanite Spring festivals, describing the love of Baal and Asherah. These interpretations proved as poor a fit as the traditional.

The breakthrough to a historical reading came in 1893 when J. G. Wetzstein, the Prussian Consul in Damascus, called attention to the nuptial rites of Syrian peasants, who have the couple, crowned, sit on a throne during the wedding feast, while guests sing them songs of praise, addressing them as "king" and "queen." Syria was only the case in point. Such customs are universal and ancient in the Nile to Oxus region.

This immediately clarified the frequent use of the word "king," and further researches along these lines identified in the formulaic phrases the standard features of oral composition. The book's style was no longer unique and bewildering, and it became possible, for the first time in 2,000 years, to read it as it had been sung.

The best critical edition incorporating modern findings is Robert Gordis' *The Song of Songs*. On this I have relied. It should be noted that all available translations suffer the influence of the *King James Version's* priggish dignity. Even Gordis', which is clear and accurate, fails to convey the simple, elegant pleasure and wit of this gallant verse.

One might half regret the historical perspective that made this translation possible. The glamour of the mystical reading is lost. Yet I think something better is gained. Restored is a humanly beautiful book which can again delight lovers, consoling their pain, inciting to new refine-

The Unholy Bible

ments of flirtation, according passion and erotic play their dignity. Going back to Rashi's or Origen's reading, one's appreciation of their work is enhanced rather than undermined, for it now becomes possible to fully savor the creativity and holy insight that discerned the patterns of the sacred in the secular. For the traditional reading is not merely a hallucination arising from the text, but, at its best, a vision of the mysteries implicit in physical love.

(1:1)

KING SOLOMON'S BOOK OF LOVE SONGS

(1: 2 – 4)

(Bride): I want to feel his mouth on mine, to drink love at his lips. The taste makes all wine weak, all liquor thin.

(Companions, addressing the Groom): Your scent is spicy rich attar, your trademark — a whiff of rich cologne. Lovesick girls breathe deep as you pass, look after you and sigh.

(Bride): Take me, draw me after you, hurry, my king, bring me to your bedroom.

(Companions, addressing the Groom): We'll dance and laugh for you! We have to admit — the bride's words make it clear — your love does more than wine. All the girls were right to fall for you.

(1: 5 – 6)

You city women, aristocratically pale, I'm beautiful even though the sun has tanned me black —

True, a Bedouin's goat-hair tent is dark as me — but so are the curtains that hang in Solomon's palace!

Don't stare at me because I'm red where the sun shot me a hot glance —

King Solomon's Book of Love Songs

I'm burnt because my brothers flared up at me, set me out here in the sun to watch over the vineyard — where no one ever comes —
They were angry that I wasn't careful enough about guarding my own orchard,
anxious lest I let the boys walk in and have a taste.

(1: 7 – 8)

Can't you tell me where you pasture your sheep, where you take them to rest in the day's heat, can't you tell me when I'm so in love with you?
Why should I wander by the flocks of your friends, looking for you?
The shepherds tell me: If you can't find your friend — a beautiful woman like you — why don't you follow the tracks of the flocks and graze your kids where we pitch our tents?

(1: 9 – 11)

Like a lordly horse, elaborate in sparkling harness, who draws a pharaoh's dazzling chariot — such is your beauty, my love,
with wide earrings of plaited gold against your cheeks, a string of coral beads around your neck.
I'll get you golden bracelets inlaid with silver studs.

(1: 12 – 14)

My king lay in bed beside me,
my perfume renewed as my skin grew warm,
my lover was like a sachet of myrrh between my breasts all night long,
like a cluster of white henna blossoms, my love, the kind that grow
by the noble vineyards of En Gedi.

The Unholy Bible

(1: 15 – 17)

(He): But you're beautiful! with your eyes as gentle and shy as doves —

(She): No you're beautiful, so sweet to me! Our bed is the new soft grass —

(He): The cedar boughs are a roof overhead, around us — a wall of pines.

(2: 1 – 3)

(She): I'm just a common wild-flower, a lily among the rocks along the valley-slope.

(He): A lily shining among rough brambles, compared to other girls.

(She): And you stand out among the boys, an apple-tree amid a forest,

I joy to sit in its shade and pleasure my palate with its fruit.

(2: 4 – 5)

He brought me to the wine-shop. His face was flushed, eyes shining love —

Bring us cakes and apples! Food! I'm fading away!

(Is it only hunger makes me feel so weak?)

(2: 6 – 7)

I rest my head on his shoulder, his arm holds me to him.

In the name of the deer and gazelles that wander through this field, by all the timid creatures shy as love,

let no strollers come upon us, let none disturb us here till Love awaken sated from its pleasure daze.

(2: 8 – 13)

I hear my lover, here he comes,

bounding down the mountainside, leaping along its rises

King Solomon's Book of Love Songs

and hillocks, barely touching the ground,
  like a gazelle or a young deer, more flying than afoot,
  — he's standing by our wall.
  peering in at the window, trying to peep through the blinds,
  (he thinks I didn't hear him!) he waits, then reveals himself with a whisper:
  "Come out, my sweet, my lovely one, no need to stay indoors,
  the Winter's heavy rains are done, the clouds have glided on,
  the land is suddenly covered in flowers, the season of song is here,
  little figs start to ripen on the tree, vine-blossoms spice the breeze.
  Come on, my dear, my beautiful, let's go!

(2: 14 – 15)

(He): "Is my little dove hiding in her high rock-crevice cliff-nest?
  Let me see your face, just hear your voice!"
(She): "Away! There's nothing left for you to pick in my vineyard,
  the vineflowers, spicing the breeze, already drew in foxes,
  young foxes have already eaten up my grapes."

(2: 16 – 17)

My lover is mine, and I am his.
I am a meadow of lilies where he grazes
  all night, till cool first morning breeze when shadows run from the sun.
  Turn again before you leave, let me look at you again,
  tall and graceful like a young deer,
  a gazelle on the mountains where spices grow.

The Unholy Bible

(3: 1 – 5)

I lie in bed, dreaming of the man I love.

Even in sleep I search for him. I cannot find him, even in a dream.

I seem to get up, to look for him through the city, along the streets, past dark shops,

my soul flies on, seeking him I love,

seeking, never finding.

Then the night-watchmen, patrolling the shadowed town, find me.

"Have you seen him, the one my soul loves?"

I float on. Suddenly he's there.

I hold him. I'll never let him go

till I bring him, hand in mine, to my mother's house,

into her own room, like a member of the family.

Quiet, quiet, Jerusalem. Women, keep the city peaceful tonight,

in the name of the deer and gazelles, by all the timid creatures shy as love,

let no sound disturb, let nothing stir me

till I awaken, sated, from my dream of love.

(3: 6 – 11)

Smoky clouds on the horizon — the dust of a caravan riding up from the desert?

It's the litter of Solomon, approaching slow, amid clouds of rising incense, of myrrh, frankincense, all the merchant's fragrant powders.

Sixty warriors surround him, Israel's heros, sword-girded, masters of battle.

These men and blades should be enough to ensure a night's quiet privacy!

King Solomon's Book of Love Songs

King Solomon had his litter made from Lebanon cedar,
the platform's plated with gold, the back and fittings silver,
the inside's upholstered in purple cloth, lovingly broidered
and tasseled
by the virgins of Jerusalem, lined with their longing.
See, girls of Zion, come look!
Solomon in the crown his mother placed on his curls
on his day of wedding and heart's joy.

(4: 1 – 7)

You're beautiful, my love. Your eyes look out, dove-gentle,
through your veil,
your hair fleeces down, thick and rich as a whole flock of
goats streaming down Mt. Gilead,
your teeth shine like a herd of sheep when they come up
from the river, white and washed for the shearing,
each one healthy and strong, like sheep that bear twins
and never miscarry.
Your lips are red like new-dyed scarlet yarn, your mouth is
gracefully fashioned, your words finely framed,
your cheeks beneath their veil blush, like the gem-red in
the white of a cut pomegranate,
your neck, adorned with a necklace of coins, is strong and
smooth like the tower David built on a height, hung round with
a thousand painted shields, necklaced with the shields of heros,
your breasts are elegant as twin gazelles grazing among
the lilies
all night, till cool first morning breeze when shadows run
from the sun.
I want to explore your myrrh-scented hills, your
frankincense slopes.
You're beautiful entirely, my love, a world of beauty,
perfect, without flaw.

The Unholy Bible

(4: 8)

You've come to me from Lebanon, my bride,
    travelled down the northern mountains — Amana, Senir, Hermon,
        from the heights where lions and panthers have their dens.

(4: 9)

With a glance, my sister, my bride,
you've hypnotised me with a glance,
with a sparkle of your necklace.

(4: 10 – 11)

Your love, my sister, is better than wine, it's made me drunk in daylight, my bride,
    your perfume's richer than all the incense,
    your words are honey — golden, sweet and slow; the taste of your lips is delicious — milk and honey are under your tongue,
    the sweep of your dress fans the air with spice
    like a breeze from Lebanon.

(4: 12 – 5:1)

(Groom): Your garden is locked, my sister, my bride, your well is closed, your fountain sealed to me —
    and it's a paradise of branching pomegranate, with sweet, precious fruit,
    with henna and spikenard, nard and saffron,
    aromatic reed, cinnamon, and all the trees with scented resin,
    myrrh and aloe, all the noble spices.
(Bride): My garden fountain's no closed well, its quick water rushes down to you like a spring in the hills of Lebanon.

King Solomon's Book of Love Songs

North wind, wake! South wind, rise! Blow through my garden, carry down its perfume
 to my love, so he'll come to my garden and taste its rarest fruit.
(Groom): I enter my garden, my sister, my bride, I pluck my myrrh and spice,
 I eat my honey from the comb, drink wine rich as milk.
(Guests): Eat, my friends, drink and be drunk with love.

(5: 2 – 6: 2)

While I slept, my heart woke to the sound of my lover
 knocking at the door of a dream.
 "Open to me, my sister, my friend, my dove, my perfect one, let me in
 — my hair is wet from cold evening mist,
 dew's dripping from my curls."
"I'm in bed — I already got out of my clothes — do I have to put them all on again?
 I just took my bath," (I continued dozily), "I don't want to get my feet dirty."
My lover began fiddling with the lock, now he took his finger from the hole,
 my heart thudded sudden, my belly tensed and trembled,
 I rose to open for him, my hands still slick and scented with myrrh from the bath-oil,
 I passed my dripping fingers along the doorbolt,
 I opened for him — he was already gone.
Not even the echo of his footsteps. My soul flew after him.
 Seeking, never finding. Calling without an answer.
 Night watchmen, patrolling the shadowed town found me
 running around in my nightgown — they thought I was a whore.
 They shoved me. They hurt me.

The Unholy Bible

The sentries who pace the city's walls, they tore off my veil
as I ran from them.

Promise me, women of Jerusalem,
if you see my lover — tell him —
tell him I'm sick from loving him so much.
"Pretty woman, what's your lover more than another?
Is he really worth our searching for him too?"
There's no one looks like him — red cheeks, a face
aristocratically pale,

his curls are dark and wild, thick like palm-branches,
black like a raven,

his eyes are bright and clear and quick,
the whites are white as a dove in the snow,
the pupils sparkle blue like a pool of icy water,
his cheeks are soft with down, like the lawn in a spice-
garden sweet with blossoming herbs,

his breath is wind through the lilies, like a breeze through
balsam trees,

his arms are columns of gold, his fingernails are gems,
his belly's carven ivory, his black chest-hair glints blue-
like lapis lazuli,

his legs are marble pillars set in bases of gold.
His glance is noble like the hills of Lebanon, he stands
like a cedar,

— his kiss is delicious.
When you see my lover you'll know it, Jerusalem women.
"Beautiful woman, where's your friend gone?
which way did he head? We're eager to help you find him."
He's gone where you can't follow, down to his garden, his bed
of spices,

to graze in the garden I keep for him, to pluck my wild-
flowers.

King Solomon's Book of Love Songs

(6: 4 – 10)

You're dazzling as Tirzah, the Northern kingdom's capitol,
 and no less splendid than Jerusalem, chief city of the
Southern realm.
 like these great towered towns you're beautiful — won-
derful — frightening.
Look away, your gaze makes me brave and insane,
 your hair fleeces down, thick and rich, like a whole goat-
flock streaming down Mt. Gilead,
 your teeth shine like a herd of sheep when they come up
from the river, white and washed for the shearing,
 each one healthy and strong, like sheep that bear twins
and never miscarry.
Solomon has sixty queens, eighty concubines, too many pretty
serving girls to count,
 — I've only one dove, one perfect one, her mother's only
daughter and special favorite
 — but one whose looks make all the girls call her lucky,
even the queens and concubines praise her:
Did the sun just rise? Who is this just came in,
 dawn-glad, sun-lovely and moon-bright, amazing, radiant,
frighteningly beautiful?

(6: 11)

I went down to my garden, wandered under the nut trees
along the stream's green banks,
 looking to see if the vine was in flower, the pomegranate in
bloom…

(line 6:12 is lost)

(7: 1 – 6)

Whirl around so we can see you, woman of Shulem;
dance, dance again, we haven't seen enough!

The Unholy Bible

Noble girl, we watch the pace and prance of your sandalled feet,
and your legs, fine formed as if a master goldsmith carved their curves.
Your navel's like a small fine shallow cup,
it doesn't need wine to excite a drunken warmth.
Your belly's smooth and white as a mound of flour, sweet as lilies,
your breasts are elegant as twin gazelles,
your neck is stately and strong, a tower of ivory.
Your eyes are like the pools at Heshbon by the gate of Bath Rabbin — glad, bright and clear to the depths.
Your nose is straight and proud as the tower of Lebanon that looks out over Damascus,
your head is majestic as Mount Carmel, your hair heavy, thick as royal purple cloth,
indeed, a king has already been caught in your curls.

(7: 7 – 9)

There's nothing so good, so delightful as Love.
Be a tall palm-tree, your breasts a cluster of dates — I'll climb to the top, hold on by the upper branches.
Your breasts are my grapes, ripe and heavy, your breath like the smell of apples, your kiss like wine: it stuns me drunk and leaves me dreaming — talking of you in my sleep.

(7: 11 – 14)

I've got a lover and he's eager for me.
Let's go to the country and sleep out in a vineyard,
wake up among the henna blossoms that grow by the grapes.
We'll see if the vines have flowered, if their buds are open yet,
whether the pomegranates are in bloom.

King Solomon's Book of Love Songs

That's where I want to make love to you.
Already by our door the aphrodisiac mandrake
gives out its subtle, irritating perfume;
outside the house the herbs have sprouted,
both last year's and those planted early this spring
— it's more than time we went out to the country.
If I've been coy, hidden my love from you,
it's because I've been saving it all for now.

(8: 1)

I wish you were my brother, that we'd sucked the same
breast,
then no one could scold me if I kissed you out in the open...
(lines 8: 2–5 are lost)

(8: 7 – 8)

Set me on your life like a seal,
tattoo my name on your wrist where the pulse is
making and marking you mine
with all your heart and all the force in your arms
— I have to utterly own,
because Love is strong like Death;
Jealousy — harsh as the Grave.
Love's fire sears like a branding iron,
burns in deeper than fever;
It splinters your life like a lightning bolt thrown by the hand
of God.
This flame you couldn't put out with a flood, rivers
couldn't wash it cold.
If a man even considered trying to buy Love
with the wealth of his entire family
— people would just walk away from him in total disgust.

(8: 8 – 10)

(Suitors): We know a little girl, too young to have breasts yet — what shall we do about our little friend when she's old enough to be courted?

If she resists, like a city wall, we'll attempt her with jewelry, silver siege-works;

if she's a closed gate, we'll storm her with carven cedar ladders, carry presents over her ramparts.

(Girl): I am a wall — to keep you out,
and I do have breasts — like towers,
stately, and beyond your reach.
But when I find the one I want to please
it is I who will besiege and conquer.

(8: 11 – 12)

Solomon has a vineyard in Baal Hamon
worth a thousand in silver yearly,
so big it costs 200 just to hire the vine-tenders.
Well, I have a little vineyard too,
whenever she's with me I'm too rich to envy
any worker's wage, or the wide estates of kings.

(8: 13 – 14)

You sit in the garden, talk with your friends, the young men.
Do they have to sit so close? You aren't whispering.
If only I could overhear you saying:
"I wish my love, tall and graceful as a young deer,
a gazelle on the mountains where spices grow,
I wish my shy love would come running past here where
I wait and watch for him."

2
Selections from *The Book of Praises*

*T**ehillim*, in English *The Book of Praises*,[1] is a hymnal assembled from collections spanning centuries. Some may actually have been written by David (c. 1000 BC) and many are clearly post-exilic (after 587 BC). Whatever their earlier employments they were all used in the liturgy of the second Temple (520 BC — AD 70), at some point during which period the book's form was fixed. The Septuagint, which differs in no material way from the Hebrew Psalter, provides a *terminus post quem* of c. 200 BC. *Psalms* is then an anthology of anthologies spanning (by the most conservative estimate) 800 years (1000 to 200 BC).

I have not translated many of the psalms. It is not their complexity but their simplicity that defeated me. These were above all *songs*, and as such would have failed had they been complex in their construction or baroque in their sense.

The richest poetry is not generally singable, nor are the best songs often, well, readable. The combination of features that make at once good songs and good poems is very rare — the songs in Shakespeare are sometimes perfect examples of this marriage of simplicity with rich content. The psalms that answer this description are here translated, but they are not many (*Psalms* 23, 137, & 126).

31

The Unholy Bible

Another type that yielded to the translator's pen were those rooted in Canaanite mythology. Here the original was literary, and so presented no great difficulties to the literary translator (*Psalm* 19).

A further reason for the untranslatable character of the psalms, beyond their songlike character, is that they are not literature but prayer. They are not poems but speeches for which the reader must supply the drama in whose context they occur. Their somewhat vague, sometimes even colorless language is meant to allow the reader to supply his own elaboration and referents. When one reads the psalms in this way, one enters, through them, almost an alternate universe: the verses stretch across the interior sky, huge and portentous as constellations. Thus entered into, in fact inhabited, by the reader, the psalms become stances, orientations, patterns of being. A true translation of such is beyond the range of a literary approach.

Still, what it was possible to translate will I hope make up in quality what it lacks in bulk, and give the reader an intelligible echo of the Jerusalem Temple cult, with its white-robed bearded Levites chanting over the gorgeous noise of drums, harps and flutes, while incense-smoke towered cloudily up and slaughtered oxen crumpled bloodily at the altar's base before a congregation of veiled women with gold bracelets clanking on their proud ankles and men with earrings and swords, the whole marble-bright gold-glaring hallelucination of Ancient Near Eastern religion, where opulence was a style of piety and excess a mode of transcendence. These poems are no simpering hymns, but court-music to be played in the Palace of God (*Psalm* 104).

The Book of Praises

19: 1 – 7[2]

The sky announces the Glory of El, the heavens' urgent
blue shouts "*He* made me!"

Each day breaks — into praises the next will repeat,

each night is a vision of how the night after will darkly
enlarge

upon El, builder of earth and sky.

Day and Night transmit all this

without speech, without words, without sound.

By darkness then light they articulate time in a harmony of
alternating reigns,

and their heavenly message reaches out to earth's furthest
verge.

At the border between night and day El set up a tent for
Shamash, the Sun-god,

who comes from it each morning, with Dawn in his arms,

like a groom striding out from under the wedding canopy
holding his new bride.

He's eager and glad as a powerful runner when the race
is about to begin,

his course is as long as from east to west

and there's nothing in between his heat doesn't reach.

23[3]

With Jah to shepherd me, I won't go hungry, I have all
things I need,

he brings me to fresh thick-grassed pastures,

there he has me rest in shade through the day's hot
hours,

he brings me where I drink from cool gentle-running
streams,

The Unholy Bible

he refreshes my soul, he leads me along the flat clear path
of Justice — which is his own and his glory.
Even if I walk down Shadow-Valley, Mot the Death-god's
realm, I'll not be scared nor need to be —
because you're with me.
It reassures me just to see the top of your staff up ahead
beyond the flock,
when I'm tired, the thought of you lifts me as a shepherd
carries a lamb.
You anoint my head with fragrances,
For me you pour wine — not a little, but till the glass runs over.
My life is a too-full cup,
gladness overflows at my eyes in tears.
Now I know that good things, goodness and love will run
to keep up with me every day of my life,
and I will live in Jah's house throughout my life's long day.

104

Jah, you are most great,
dressed in splendor and majesty,
your clothing is the light.
You built the heavens to be your house —
your palace is the sky.
The clouds are your horse
whose wings are the wind.
The breezes are your messengers,
lightning bolts — your servants.
You made the earth a firm and forever unshakable place.
You pulled the floodwaters over it like a blanket,
covering mountaintops — and at your shout
they rushed back down, running from your thunder.
As the waters drew off, hills rearose,
valleys sank, all went back to the place you first gave it.

The Book of Praises

You made the shores a border
the waters can't repass to recover the earth.
You set springs in the mountains to feed into streams
then rivers torrenting through gorges
to where they give drink to the beasts of the plain,
quenching the thirst of the wild ass,
watering riverbank trees —
home to birds who sing among the leaves.
You lean out of heaven's high window
and pour rain on the green mountaintops.
You feed the entire world,
make grass for cattle to crop and crops for men to tend
you have earth sprout grain for bread
that restores a man's strength, and the vine
that gladdens hearts, makes faces glow.
You nourish the cedars of Lebanon
which you planted to be the trees of God:
their branches host all birds —
the stork makes his house in the highest.
You formed the crag-paths — easy roads for the goat,
and rocky hillsides where the rabbit makes his castle.
You shaped the moon to mark months,
and the sun who never forgets what time it is,
you bring down dark — it's night.
Forest animals come slinking out.
The lion roars for bloody meat,
calling for God to send him a kill.
Sun rises — they're all gathered back
creeping to their lairs.
Man goes out to his work,
busy with it till evening comes.
How great are your creations, Jah!
How wisely you made them,

The Unholy Bible

everywhere the earth shows your work.
Here and huge is the sea, holding the land in its blue and
limitless hands,
cupping infinities of fish, from microscopic to big as the
ships
that to and fro across it,
and Leviathan, who you gave the whole ocean to play in.
All these creatures look only to you to feed them every day.
You give — they gather their dinner.
Your hand is open — they gorge on good things.
You hide your face — they feel death-fear,
you take back their breath — they die, they're dirt.
You breathe in life, the land's refreshed,
recreatured with newborn things.
God is glorious forever! May he delight in his creations!
If he just looks at earth it quakes,
if he touches the mountains they volcano out smoke.

(lines 33–35, a pious gloss, omitted).

137

By the rivers of Babylon, it was there we were allowed to
rest; when we'd reached the shores of the Tigris and
Euphrates, then we found time for tears.
The harps we'd brought with us — what was left from the
Temple's wreck — these we leaned against the riverside trees,
we sat on the bank and wept for what had been Zion.
Then our Babylonian captors demanded music,
commanded us to act glad, saying:
"Sing us one of your Jew songs!"
With what cheer could we sing the songs of Jah
kidnapped to this new shore?

The Book of Praises

Jerusalem! If I ever forget you may I have a stroke!

May my right arm be paralysed, my tongue forget how to speak —

if Jerusalem isn't still more to me than any pleasure,

and no pleasure true or real that I can't share with her.

Remember, Adonai, what Edom did, how they helped Babylon's armies,

don't forget Jerusalem's last day, when they shouted: "Plough it under,

tear out Jerusalem's rocks by the roots!"

And Babylon, God remembers you,

Babylon about to fall.

Lucky! whoever gets to do to you what you did to us,

who'll seize *your* children and smash them against rocks.

126

When God returned us to our land from Babylon

we stopped at every step, looked back, and thought it was a dream.

Then it was our turn to laugh.

The goyim said: "Their God really does exist,

look what he's done for them."

We cried: "Jah, bring us back from exile

to the land that thirsts for our return as the desert waits for rain."

He answered: "Who sows the seeds, watering the unborn plants with tears

will roar with joy, harvesting the fullgrown grain.

Though now he staggers out to the fields, full seed-sack on his back, groaning over every furrow,

he surely will return, holding triumph-high his sheaves, rejoicing in the very weight of them."

3
How?

Cries of the Prophet Jeremiah over the City of God
fallen to the armies of Babylon in the year 587 BC

The title *How?* is a literal translation of the first word in the text, for in Hebrew, as in Arabic, books take their titles from their first significant word.

Traditionally, *How?* is ascribed to the Prophet Jeremiah. This is most unlikely, due to the highly, almost affectedly literary style, and the positive attitude towards the royal house. It is nonetheless, by my reading, the work of a single author: though the book is full of philosophic inconsistencies and shifts of position, an overriding logic prevails: it is the portrait of a soul, completed by its own contradictions.

Further, the book functions as a whole. It begins with a historically panoramic, almost aerial view of ravaged Judah, focussing in on the figure of grieving Jerusalem. Chapter 2 cuts to the calamity itself, the siege and fall of the city as seen first-hand, recounted in grim unsparing detail. In Chapter 3 the author speaks in the first person, and as we see through his eyes we enter into his soul where coexist the extremes of faith and despair that explode into the book's most terrific insights, peaking with the question:

The Unholy Bible

Don't Good and Evil both come into being because of towering Jah?

This glimpse of the amoral vastness of God, who cannot be suspected of being anything so limited as "good" or "evil," is immediately clouded over by the iconography of the sky-god and his justice — the one idolatry the Hebrew genius always allows itself. But the realisation, once made, cannot be retreated from — as Job will show.

Chapters 4 and 5 move slowly back through the aftermath, into the occupation. In contrast to the rage of 1 and 2, these chapters, in the wake of the understanding achieved in 3, are soft, solemn and dirge-like, moving through sorrow to longing, a movement which ends in an address to God that is the plea and song of a lover.

I

How can I comprehend? The overcrowded city now full of emptiness, totally alone,
on the ground like a widow sitting shiva.
She was more like a nation than a city, greater than other *countries*, a master to her provinces. Today she became a slave.
She cries and cries in the night, tears drip from her chin.
Of all who said they loved her no one's there to comfort her.
All her friends — just left her, became her enemies.
Judah's gone into exile after so much struggle and pain.
Even while she held her land, a nation among nations, she was never secure, was never let lower her guard —
and all her enemies moved against her when she was trapped between the foreign powers as in a narrowing pass.
Zion's roads are deserted tracks, bare paths no one travels gladly,
all her gates hang open as if they were stunned,
the priest's every breath comes out as a sigh,

How?

the Temple virgins feel it like a sickness in their guts. Grief beats on Zion.

Her haters are in control now; her enemies take it easy, since Jah himself makes her suffer for how rotten she was, her enemies watch their prisoners — her children — led away.

The lady Zion doesn't feel so beautiful now, she's lost that high commanding glamour of hers;

her princes, arrogantly graceful as stags, they're like starving deer who can't find any pasture,

without enough strength to run from the hunter.

Jerusalem understands what pain is now. That point is driven home as she's driven from her home.

She remembers all her precious things — they'd always been hers, by right —

as the enemy's hand clamps onto her shoulder. And she has no help.

The attacker knows it and laughs to see her fall.

Jerusalem did evil — that's why she became a thing to shrink from, loathsome as a menstruous rag;

whoever respected her despises her now. They know she's a slut. They've *seen* her cunt.

She drops to her knees with a groan and hits the ground with her palms.

Her skirts are caked and stained. She never gave a damn what would happen,

till the moment she fell like no one else had ever — and there was none to help her.

(She says): "Look, Jah, see how my pain makes the enemy proud."

The one who comes against her grabs and handles all her fine things, the things she loved.

She watched the goyim walk into her Temple's inmost sanctuary —

The Unholy Bible

you ruled no gentile should ever go in there even to pray!

The entire people search for bread even as they mourn,

they give their jewels for enough food to almost keep them alive.

(Jerusalem says): "Look Jah, consider. I know I'm worthless, I should be thrown away.

"All you people passing by: go every road, look, reflect,

whether anyone's ever been cut down with wound or sickness like mine

which God sent down upon me in white-hot annihilating rage.

"He fired his lightning from the high vast gap of heaven, sent it jagging and flashing into my bones.

He buried landmines for my feet, I was hurled away. It was horribly amazing.

I'm sick with terrible menstrual cramps all day long.

"They watch my every step for a chance to administer a kick;

God clamped a yoke around my neck, my strength is caving in.

Leader of leaders and God of gods, he handed me over to those I can't stand up to.

"God my master has made a heap of my strong men and warriors — all of them.

He declared a harvest festival in the midst of me, he gave a party in my dishonor, to bash my firstborn males like grapes.

I was Adonai's beautiful Judah — he stamped me out like in a winepress.

"My eye overflows,

there is no help, for this.

My sons are in a stupor, the enemy won!"

Zion holds out her hands — for nothing.

Jah passed sentence on Jacob, enemies were around to hear it.

How?

Jerusalem falls at their feet and grasps their knees — they shove her away in disgust.

(She says): "God is just! I did wrong, I rebelled against Jah. Listen, all peoples, see how he hurt me,

sending my daughters and sons into exile.

"I shouted to my lovers for help — they betrayed me;

my priests and elders died in the city

feebly foraging food.

"Look Jah, I'm becoming a corpse, hot lava oozes brutal through my bowels,

my mind is altered within me. I know! I did wrong! I rebelled against Jah!

Outdoors it is the sword, at home the survivors sit silent as the dead.

"I cannot speak. I exhale sickly cooings, mournful noises. There is no help.

Enemies heard of my disaster, they're overjoyed you did it,

— but you bring the day you warn of, they'll all become. like me.

"Bring together, consider all their crimes, break *them* in pieces

and crush their remnants just like you did to me for my offenses,

making me pay with groans and cries and a sick heart's halting beats."

II

How could Adonai cover himself in black anger clouds

darkening day to Zion, closing the heavens against her prayers and cries?

— how could he thunder down the skyish towers of his beautiful city, Israel's glory — how could the Temple itself, his

The Unholy Bible

footstool, the entry-point of his presence in the world, mean nothing to him anymore — how could he kick these down and stamp them flat on his day of wrath?

Adonai swallowed up the homes of Jacob's people,

exploding, he tore down the fortresses of beautiful Judah, made rooftop touch ground,

he made the kingdom a junkyard, the princes derelicts.

In smoking vehemence combust he cut off all of Israel's strength as one might saw the horns off a bull,

tied Israel's hands behind his back and left him for the enemy,

cremated Jacob with a lightning bolt, left a smoking crater around the remains.

Our enemy, he bent his bow against us; murderous, he held it steady, took grim deliberate aim

and shot down all our warriors, young beautiful men,

his flickering ire outburst upon the tent of fine Zion in vomiting fire,

a ruthless Adonai unbuilt Israel,

a hard God shattered the castles, broke the strongholds open,

made all Judah groan.

He tore up the Temple's enclosure like a garden, rooted out the places of sacred observance,

Jah made Sabbath and Holidays fade away from Zion,

the names of priest and king had no more meaning here.

Adonai knocked over his altar and dragged down his temple,

opened to enemies the palace walls,

there was shouting in the house of God — it sounded like a festival being held.

Jah decided to havoc the walls of shining Zion,

with surveyor's tools he took careful measure and set about to un-make.

How?

The ramparts paled, the stones whitened like a sepulchre
— a wailing wall —
The bars cracked and flew as the city gates fell slowly
heavily flat and thud to ground;
kings and princes away in foreign lands, none led,
if we still had a future, not even the prophets could see it.
The elders of Zion sit silent on the ground,
they've wrapped themselves in coarse cloth as mourners,
they pour dirt on their heads,
Jerusalem's women double over with woe, their hair trails
in the dust.
My eyes are swollen from tears, my stomach aches with
grief,
I'm retching up my liver at the hurt of this people I love,
for the children, babies, fainting in the city street.
They ask their mothers for bread, for drink,
— like wounded men they pass out right in the street,
their breathing ceases in their own mothers' laps.
What can I compare this to, how begin to understand
what's happened to you, my bright Jerusalem?
Dear Zion, can any word of mine encompass, to calm,
your grief?
Can a man lift the sea in his cupped hands, or heal a shattered stone?
Your prophets saw what you wanted them to see,
none told you truth about yourself to turn back the order
for your exile.
They daubed your faults with whitewash, made insipid
allowances for everything, till you became a rotten wall held
together by layers of paint.
Now everyone who passes claps their hands,
shakes their head and whistles at fine Jerusalem.
"So *this* is the city they called 'Earth's Joy' and 'Beauty

The Unholy Bible

Utterly Achieved'?"

Your enemies laugh over you, they show you their back teeth,

they hiss and gibber to get your attention, then say: "We *buried* you!"

This is the day we *waited* for — we really lived to see it!"

As God planned, so did God enact, what he said he has made happen,

just as long before he swore, he smashed and didn't pity,

he used you to glad your enemies — he backs up all their brag.

Call to God with all your mind sweet grieving Zion,

pour out your entire heart under God's gaze in a flood,

lift your hands to him, reach out and beg for your children's lives.

Look Adonai, see who you did this to,

should starving women eat their young, the babies they nursed?

Should prophet and priest be murdered in the Temple of God?

The boys and elders lie on the ground, in the street,

young women, young men — both felt the sword.

You were angry and you killed, cold butcher God.

You summoned the enemies awaiting this chance, invited them as if to a feast,

no one escaped, no one fled Adonai's day of wrath.

Our children were only raised to be destroyed.

III

I am the man who watched while angry God raised his pastoral staff against us and threw it like a spear —

the Lord my shepherd lead me, sent me off — into night and nowhere.

How?

He turned against me too, that long destroying day.

My bones were showing under wasted muscle, thinning skin — he broke them.

I have nothing left. I can go nowhere else. All around me, Impossibility, a wall.

Am I dead and is this nothingness, the God-apart noplace dark?

God walled me in, made heavy my chain. I won't be leaving here.

My shouts and cries of prayer, shut out, echo senseless back.

Buildings' rubble and wall-collapse fill every impassible path.

Like a bear, God waited silent for me; a lion, he slunk from behind,

misled me, then tore into me, suddenly gutted and gored,

he set me up — like a target, bent bow, sighted down the arrow —

he speared my kidneys with his quiver's whole payload.

The peoples of the world laughed and told each other Jew-jokes.

God knew how to glut my gut with nausea and stuff my face with pain.

He stamped on my back as I lay in the dirt, ground my mouth in the gravel.

Safety, Peace, Happiness? Were those words I'd ever used?

I felt myself ending; I'd lost my hope in God.

Memory sours the tongue in my mouth, I flinch to think how we fled,

remembering how we're hurt, the soul inside me shrinks down low.

But there's one thing I keep dragging back to mind, that gives me strength to wait:

The Unholy Bible

God's mercy and love do *not* run out, they *cannot* come to an end,

each morning proves they've been renewed and like the earth they're sure,

and *nothing* can take my God from me! and therefore I have hope.

For God *is* good to the soul that trusts, the soul that asks of him,

it's right to wait patient, silently, for help and rescue from Jah,

it's best to get humble and neck-bent accept this yoke while you're still young —

then when it presses heaviest you'll sit unprotesting alone,

you'll prostrate yourself face-flat before God, then — damn right you have reason to hope!

You'll offer your chin to the fist and accept as God-sent all contempt.

God won't reject forever his own.

If he hits, he will pity — because he loves.

He takes no joy in hurting and humbling human beings.

To kick the face of all on earth who are already in chains,

To subvert a man's case with courtroom distortions goes clash against the nature of most high Jah,

when human rights are wronged God looks most undelighted on.

And whose order was it brought into being all that is *as it is?*

Who was it made the world with a word, who was it "spoke and it was?"

Don't Good and Evil both come into being because of towering Jah?

How dare a human find fault with the Cosmos, complain he's punished too much?

How?

Let him think what he is, what he's done, what deserved
— in spite of which he *lives*.

Let's examine the path we chose and explore whether we
can follow it back to God.

Reach out in utmost offering of self, arms held out to God
in the sky, stretch out in supplication, hold out your hearts in
your hands.

Yes! we did wrong, we disobeyed you — and you, you
didn't forgive.

You cast your anger over us like a net, hunted us down,
red untender God,

you sealed yourself off in your clouds and wouldn't listen
to prayers,

you threw us out among the nations like garbage.

Our enemies make faces at us, grown giddy with sated hate,

as I watch a thrill of terror goes through me to the balls, it's
like looking down from a cliff — only here the fear's as real
as the corpses and rubble —

I'll stand and cry over my sweet people till the tears eat a
hole in the ground,

my hot eyes overflow, they'll never close or cool

till God, hidden in his heaven, again looks down to us.

Even if I could stand to, tears won't let me see more.

I'd done nothing. They trapped me like an animal, a bird,

I could almost hear the dirt down-clatter across my cof-
fin's lid.

I sank towards Sheol, world of the Dead, its heavy black
waters flowed over my head.

Out of my grave I call your name, Adonai!

Listen Jah, you hear me! Rescue and help!

Be present to me when I cry to you, tell me not to be scared,
take my side and save my life;

just judge, see how I'm harmed,

The Unholy Bible

watch their malicious deliberate cruelty.
Smell the stink of their scheming against me, Jah,
all day long they hatch up slanders to blame something
new on the Jew,
my sufferings are their morning song, by night their lullaby.
Pay them back what they've earned, O God, full wage for
finished work,
let their crazed brains bake with irrational hate to surely
earn your curse,
hunt them down to nothing, annul them from under the sky.

IV

Is it possible gold can tarnish, or silver lose its worth?
precious stones left lying in the street?
Yet Zion's golden children are thrown away like paper.
The desert jackal will offer her teat and give the cub suck,
but my people's women have lost even that brute and common tenderness,
they're like the desert ostrich
that lays and leaves its eggs on the ground to be crushed
under every foot.
Thirst glues the forgotten babe's tongue to its palate.
The children ask for bread — none have it to give.
The ones who fed on gourmet morsels are out on the street
in a daze,
brought up in silk, they sleep in garbage heaps.
Jerusalem must have done worse than Sodom to deserve
this —
that city fell in an instant, none knew the hand that struck.
Our young nobles with milky uncalloused skin, glaringly
beautiful as snow, with a fine ruddy blush upon them as of
polished coral,
pearl-pale from the luxuried indoor life, made of some finer

How?

stuff than mortal, graceful as figures carved on a gem —

blackened out of recognition with filth, they're shadows, nameless and non,

hunger's made dry sticks of their limbs, their shrunk eathery skin wrinkles in at each exhale.

Luckier, those gored with the sword than those gutted by hunger the whole siege long,

at least they died with their bellies full, faced death in their strength.

With their own hands mothers cook their children for meat, feed upon it, waiting for the city to crack.

The outer wall burst like a dam — hot rubble and glowing smoke — the wrath of Jah in burning surf ploughed fire into Zion.

At first no country or government on earth believed a foreign army could march

through the gates of the city of God.

Because of your lies, you prophets! your crimes, you priests!

who said nothing while just men's blood was shed right out in the street.

You totter along the roads, your own blood caked on your robes,

what you once couldn't bear to hear of, today you wear.

In your torn grungy clothes people take you for lepers. "Unclean!" they shout, "Don't touch! Get away!"

You run from place to place, country to country. No nation takes you in, none let you stay.

You Levites, God and his Temple were your inheritance, your territory and portion among the tribes.

Once God set you apart for his own — now he can't stand the sight of you.

And you're no reverend men to the conqueror either. Your

The Unholy Bible

years and dignities get no respect from them.

All night we strained our gaze at the blackness, for help that would come from Egypt,

leaning from the watchtowers, seeing shapes in shadows, hearing hope in every sound.

Now the Babylonian garrisons cut down anyone found in our streets.

This is what came of all our brave patience, this is what it earned.

The King and his guard escaped the city by night. Babylon vaulted after them like an eagle sky-diving from topmost cloud,

hunted them down the mountains, trapped them in Jericho's plain.

Zedekiah, God's anointed king, taken. An earthquake had done no more.

While he stood for us we'd have sheltered in his shadow and lived.

Dance, laugh, Edom, descendants of cheated Esau, who've lain in wait for us forever in the desert far south, who joined Babylon marching up against Jerusalem.

The cup we drink will yet come round to you, you too will stagger as we do now, like us you're "gonna get wrecked."

Zion, your punishment's come and done, this is indeed the exile long foretold.

But Edom! God's still adding up your crimes, none hidden, none forgot.

V

O God, do not forget us, see how low we're beaten down. Haven't we fallen far enough by now?

The land you gave, taken away, strangers settled in our homes. Widow-guardless, orphan-weak, we have no safety more.

How?

We sip water for a price, the last possessions go for a little wood and warmth.

The yoke is on our necks. We're worked like animals.

Our parents had no trust in Jah, they allied with Assyria, pacted with Egypt, lived well on the blood of those to be — of us, who pay the cost of their contempt for God, who bear the day they thought would never come.

Babylon's slaves master us, their petty officials king it where we live.

A piece of bread can cost your life. You only live because some soldier's sword-arm's tired.

Our limbs have blackened, shriveled in the oven of hunger.

They rape our women, trap and grapple our daughters.

They hang our princes and leaders. The aged are honored with a kick.

The young men turn the mill, tied to it like mules, else they stumble under loads of wood and stone.

No more, the old men at the city gate, arguing politics, rendering opinions. No more, the boys running through with their games and songs.

No more, the gladdened heart. The dance becomes a sullen trudge of mourners, dull, reluctant, looking down.

God's light and leading taken like a crown from our heads — Oy! that we ever disobeyed Jah!

For this our heart is weak and sick, *this* darkens day to us: the God-apartness and the big Alone.

You, Jah! Will you go on battering us forever down? Will every generation cringe beneath?

Were we never yours, that you can cut and cast us eternally away?

Let us be close again, Adonai, we wait for you alone! Let us live, as once, for you, our God who makes us live at all.

We can bear your fury — not to feel you far.

4
JOB

*T*he *Book of Job* is generally placed in the post-exilic period, somewhere in the 4th–3rd centuries BC. Many arguments have been made for this on stylistic grounds, but the most convincing is that of the historical context suggested by the book's content. In the period when Israel had lost its land for two generations, and its autonomy forever, the confident, patriotic God-concept of the Kingdom period was no longer tenable: in the ruins of Royal ambitions, luridly and implausibly aglow with the eschatologic fantasies of the later prophets, we see the most appropriate setting for the skeptical Wisdom literature of *Job* and *Ecclesiastes*. To us, who have in this century seen the wreck of so many hopes, systems and syntheses, these grimly disabused writings may offer the most congenial and immediate voice of all.

There is no part of *Job* that has not been rejected as spurious by someone. We adopt a very conservative reading in rejecting only the speeches of Elihu, which will be summarised and discussed after the translation itself.

The action takes place in a foreign country, somewhere in the East: this is analogous to the setting of Roman comedies in Greece with slaves as protagonists — the establishment of distance makes it possible for Job to make comments which

The Unholy Bible

would have been too outrageous in the mouth of a Jew.

I would read the prologue as existential absurdity — suffering *doesn't* make any sense, and the bet with Satan takes wry cognizance of this fact.

The action itself is relatively straightforward. Job is, and remains, blameless — we have the prologue and epilogue, his own statements, and God's acknowledgement to corroborate this. His friends insist that God is perfectly just, that if Job is punished he must have done something wrong. Job's position is that he himself is perfectly just, and that God is behaving immorally by punishing him. God's reply is that he is neither moral nor immoral, but rather *amoral*.

The most interesting thing about the book is that everyone is in some degree right. The friends are wrong in their assessment of Job, but their descriptions of the world as ruled by a reliably retributive justice are in the main correct — not to any extent that will satisfy those who suffer unjustly; but the fact that we continue to accept existence is proof that most people feel the world's sufficiently fair. It would be difficult to find a successful person who didn't agree in large part with the friends.

Job's position is fascinatingly untenable. He embodies the contradictions of the Hebrew Sky-god concept.[4] On the one hand the Sky-god's implications of Totality, enormously reinforced by his status as supreme deity, make God responsible for *all* that occurs — and so Job correctly blames God for his suffering. On the other hand, the sky-god is characteristically the establisher of the norms of existence — the origin of all fairness and justice. Thus Job is similarly justified in appealing to God for justice — even against God.

The Hebrews were almost unique in not devaluing the Sky-god concept in the face of the very contradictions Job encounters. Job's heroic action is not, as is generally sup-

Job

posed, his patience, (of which he gives little evidence) but his extraordinary *loyalty* to a conception of God as both all-powerful and entirely fair, despite the fact it does not match reality. He complains of God, but never meaningfully questions or rejects him — Job remains God's loyal opposition.

God himself is typologically a very curious phenomenon: Job addresses him in typical sky-god language, invoking his omniscience, justice, totality, &c., often with explicitly sky imagery — clouds, sunlight, etc. The theophany is startlingly different. This God is neither, like Canaanite El, the sky god, nor is he become, despite certain attributes (the hurricane he speaks out of, his boast of how he subdued the original chaos), Baal the storm god — the typical replacement of the sky-god for the disillusioned Hebrew. The concept we have here is rather like what one calls the Master of the Animals, an order of deity who is associated with Paleolithic hunter-gatherer society, and who guarantees the well-being and fecundity of (particularly animal) life, and has no especial concern with humans — this is a god neither of the sky nor of the land, but of the superabundance of life, the cosmic generosity.

We should not be misled by the question format in God's reply to Job: this is merely rhetorical, and is not directed at revealing Job's want of knowledge, but only serves to frame the irony of God's explaining himself to man. *The content of the speech is exclusively to describe God as the source of all animal life* (note that man has no special mention here).

Is the answer satisfactory? In a moral sense, and on human terms, no. This is not however the bitter wit of a Euripides *deus ex machina*, aiming to show you how hopeless and awful it is to exist. There is an important amelioration of God's gigantic flippancy: his acknowledgement that Job was right (or at least not wrong). From this emerges a rather heroic and humanist image of man, whom even God must

The Unholy Bible

acknowledge, as the source of meaning and morality in the face of God's own chaotic and amoral opulence. The view of life is very much like Nietzsche's, or even Pindar's.

If this disappoints our sense of fairness, it should not our sense of truth. The epilogue does not betray this — rather it presents a facile conclusion to satisfy those who can't grasp the harsher satisfactions the text offers. But there are cues — like the syrupy names given Job's daughters and God's rebuke to the friends — that it's meant tongue in cheek. In a sense the prologue and conclusion are, with their fairy-tale character, an overview of the whole book: the ambiance of the fairy-tale is the only non-tragic way of bringing together the divine and human points of view. And it must be borne in mind that *Job* is structurally a comedy: one may justly see in it the dinosauric prototype of Jewish humor.

JOB

(1)

There was once a man named Job who lived far away in the East, a blameless, upright man who stood in reverent awe of God and refused to do wrong. He had seven sons and three daughters ; his holdings came to 7,000 sheep, 3,000 camels, 500 teams of oxen and 500 she-asses; his was an enormous estate, in fact the largest in the East.

Now when holidays came around his sons took turns hosting the feast, each inviting all the others over to share the pleasures of the day. Whenever one of these feasts approached, Job sent for his children, blessed them, and ritually purified them of any sins they might have incurred, offering for each an atonement sacrifice (though in fact his children were as blameless as he), taking this extra precaution because, he rea-

Job

soned, "they might have committed a sin unawares or offended God by an ill-considered thought." Job never failed to take these careful measures.

One day when the gods were assembled before their creator — among them the Accuser — God turned to the Slanderous Seraph and asked:

"What have you been up to?"

"Oh, wandering around the earth, travelling the planet."

"Did you happen to notice my servant Job? I'll bet you've nothing to say against that unexampled man — blameless, upright, ever in reverent awe of God, refusing to do wrong."

"Don't you make sure it pays to act like that? Isn't your protection around him like a fortified wall? around him, his family, all he has? You see to it whatever he does succeeds: his livestock breeds till it overflows the plains! But if you used your power *against* his possessions, so much as touched his stuff — see if he wouldn't curse you to your face.

Jah said to the Accuser:

"I'll put all he has in your power, but him you leave alone, don't even —"

The Accuser was already gone.

It was a holiday. Job's daughters and sons were feasting and drinking at the home of the eldest.

A man ran up to Job.

"Your oxen were plowing, with the asses grazing nearby — and a band of nomads attacked, murdered the herdsmen, stole the animals. I'm the only one who got away — "

While he was still speaking another man ran up:

"A thunderbolt burned up all your flocks and shepherds. I'm the only one who got away — "

While he was still speaking another man ran up:

"Your sons and daughters were feasting and drinking wine at the home of your eldest and a gale came in over the desert

The Unholy Bible

and blew the house down on top of them and they're all dead. I'm the only one who got away."

Job arose and performed the formal rites of mourning: tore his garments, shaved his head and beard, fell to the ground stretched out in flat submission to the will of God. He said:

"When I came out of my mother's womb I was naked and I had nothing.

Naked, having nothing, I'll be buried, returned to the womb of my mother earth.

Nothing a man has is really his — Jah lends, takes back again. Jah is holy and glorious forever."

In all, Job's conduct was flawless.

(2)

The next day when the gods were assembled before their master, the Accuser made a point of being there too.

God turned to the Slanderous Seraph and said:

"What have you been up to?"

"Wandering the earth, travelling the planet."

"Did you happen to notice my servant Job — that unexampled man — blameless, upright, ever in reverent awe of God, refusing to do wrong,

who holds on hard to his blameless ways even though at your enticement I ruined his life for no reason at all?"

"So he accepts the loss — he figures its his ransom and as such cheap enough. They paid, he's safe. But if it's his hide takes the beating from the hand of God — then see if he doesn't curse you to your face."

Jah said:

"His body's in your power — just don't kill him."

The Accuser hit Job with a horrible skin disease from the soles of his feet to the top of his scalp so that all Job could do

Job

was sit on the ground scratching himself with a potsherd.

His wife said:

"Are you still holding on hard to your blameless ways? Curse God! If he kills you he'll be doing you a favor."

Job answered:

"You speak like a fool and a woman. Should we accept the will of God only when he does what we want?"

Job's reply was morally flawless.

When Job's three friends Eliphaz, Bildad and Zophar heard of all the sufferings that had befallen Job, they gathered from their respective countries and went together to visit him, to sympathise and comfort him.

From a distance they didn't even recognize him. When they realized who it was they groaned and wept, rubbed dirt in their hair, tore their clothing and were spectacularly aggrieved. They sat on the ground beside him for seven days and nights, in silence, respecting his agony.

(3)

Finally Job opened his mouth, to curse his birthday:

The day I was born, when they said "It's a boy!" — may that day with its night cease to exist,

in that day's place be a black unlit space, and God never peer down from heaven to look for it with the sun's searchlight.

May that day drown in its own night! Let Death inherit the date and mark it for his own with heavy low cloud, drizzle, mist and eclipse, every chilling thing that deadens day,

and may its night be starless thick and dull, moonless to show it's been disowned by the lunar calendar too —

may there be no begetting on that night so sadly black it scares numb the thought of bed-pleasure and the joys that darkness otherwise invites,

The Unholy Bible

may the witches who know how to summon up sleeping Leviathan, put out the sun and draw down the moon, may they nail the day with a curse

so the morning star never shines through shadows to announce it. It'll stay one day-long predawn dark, a pointless wait for a dawn that never raises rose eyelid over sun's gold eye.

Because on that day the womb ejected me, exposed me to pain and grief,

because I didn't die right then, breathing my first and last.

Why was I ever accepted by a mother's arms, why was I given a breast to suck?

I'd be lying quiet now, safe and dead, untroubled and asleep,

along with the kings and ministers of history whose palaces and actions are just rumors and ruins now,

with the rich men and princes who stockpiled gold and filled their homes with silver;

luckier still to be a buried abortion, a stillborn that never opened eye — not even to have been!

There the evil finally leave off their malicious industry, there all the exhausted can at last relax,

there even a slave is allowed to sleep late — he'll hear no master's shout.

Big-shots, nobodies, all there, all the same, none serve and no-one's boss.

Why is light given to those who've seen enough, breath to those who hate life?

who pray for death and it doesn't come, who search out ways to the grave like it was buried treasure,

who are so relieved when they can finally die they perish squealing in helpless bliss.

Why does God keep giving more existence to a man when he's lost to life, when his path has disappeared, faded out from

Job

underfoot and God's blockaded any way back to happiness?

My mouth has forgotten how to eat — so long the only thing in it's been the groans that pour through me like water.

All I feared, was scared might happen, I was right to dread, it's here.

I used to stay awake taking anxious pains, exhausted myself with precautions,

and now it's the terror of what's already happened that doesn't let me rest.

(4)

Eliphaz relied:

I'm going to try and tell you something. I hope you're up to hearing it — but no-one can listen to this kind of talk and answer nothing back.

Lots of times I've heard you lecture slumping defeated people, set them straight and toughen them up,

a foot-dragging head-down man came marching back from your reprimand.

— but when you're the one that's hit you can't accept it — when it touches you, you panic,

because you trusted too much in your piety, figured nothing bad could happen to a man pure as you.

Have you ever heard of an innocent man's having been destroyed? When was a righteous people ever wiped out?

So far as I know, that's what happens to the wicked — they have to harvest as bad as they planted and planned.

God obliterates them with a blast of anger.

Those lions that preyed on the people roar, outraged and helpless — God's kicked in their teeth,

they can't make any more killings, they starve and their cubs are scattered.

The Unholy Bible

Listen to this insight that came upon me quiet as a whisper from behind —

in the hour when all sink deepest into sleep I was still half-thinking half-dreaming —

Fear jolted my bones.

Cold wind blew across my face, my every hair bristled.

Something stood there, I couldn't make it out,

a shape facing me. Silence, then a voice:

Can a man be right and God wrong? a human more perfect than the one who made him?

God can't even put full trust in the angels: celestial spirits err!

Then what about a being that inhabits a frame of clay, who's nothing but dust,

one could crush him like a moth,

created and crumbled during one day's light, gone forever before he's even noticed,

vanished as fast as a tent collapses when the main peg's pulled —

how wise can a human be, how much can he have learned in the instant he was given to live?

(5)

Go on, complain, present your appeal — to whom? what god will side with you against God?

Being indignant won't help you here — you know the proverb: "His own anger is what gets a fool killed."

I've seen just such an overconfident arrogant fool, rooted firm in wealth and success, lose it all in an instant,

his kids had no one to turn to — they were cheated in business, defrauded in the courts,

and all the greedy people who'd stared hungry at his fields

Job

now stripped them to the stubble, sniffed out all he'd stored and gulped it gone.

Trouble like that doesn't sprout from the ground for no reason like a weed.

Man's born to earn and deserve his misery — it's his nature — he heads for harm sure as sparks fly up when you stir the fire.

Even so, I'd still try to find a way back to God, I'd make my prayer to him,

he does more great amazing things than man will ever explore, miracles more than one could count,

he gives the earth its morning dew and the fields their share of rain.

He takes poor men at sorrow's low point and rescues, sets them high;

he makes schemers' plans fail so nothing they set their hands to works,

trips them up with their own cleverness, sends them spinning out of control.

They never know they're lost: in noon's light they're still in the dark — blind men tapping for the path.

Meanwhile God leads their victims out of range of their lawyers and swords,

so the weak have hope and the evil have to just shut up.

Look, you're lucky when God punishes you — he's teaching you, don't turn away,

if he slices into you he'll bandage the wound, the hands that hurt will heal you.

Nine times out of ten God rescues, and in that tenth case you won't even be at risk,

he'll feed you through famine, save from the sword in wartime,

no liar's tongue will dare begrudge your luck or attack you sitting secure,

The Unholy Bible

you'll laugh at the threat of hunger, marauders, wild
animals,

the very fields will be your allies, their rocks will shift position to avoid your plough, no pest will nibble your grain,

you'll know all's well in your tents, never find a
thing missing when you overview your holdings.

You'll plant a family growing up countless and quick as
the wheat in your field.

You'll approach your grave still strong but ready for death,
like a crop that stands tallest at harvest-time.

So far as we could find out, this is the way things are —
now you listen up and learn it.

(6)

Job answered:

If only scales could calculate my rage, tabulate the weight
of my pain —

but it's heavier now than the sodden sand of every beach on
earth — when I try to heave it into speech all I can do is gag.

God pinned me with his poisoned arrows — their venom
spreads through my soul like a stain, panic lays me flat.

No jackass brays when he's got good grass to chomp, no
bull bellows with his face in the manger

— but I can't dummy up and suck down your no-salt
mush of platitudes insipid as eggwhite slime,

the mind refuses even to taste such sickly milktoast drivel.

If only someone granted me what I ask for, if only God
gave me what I'm hoping for —

if only he'd be good enough to crush me, let loose and kill
me with a quick fist,

that would console me despite all that's happened, I'd
laugh as I spasmed out of being. Just don't mercifully spare
my life any longer!

Job

I'll nevermore dispute the decree of God if he answers me in a fast death sentence.

What power do you imagine is mine that I'd have strength to go on hoping? And what's waiting for me in the end that I should further strain my soul waiting to see it?

Is mine the endurance of rock? Is my flesh made out of bronze?

What hope could I have wisely helped myself with that hasn't been beaten out of me?

A dying man expects kindness from his friends, not to have his piety criticized,

but my friends cheat me — like a river you see overflowing its banks, rushing down from the mountains dark and cold from melting snow, but as soon as it's summer that ice-water's gone, translated into mist and mud, then just a few trickles twisting down the riverbed and disappeared into the desert,

caravans and nomads trusted to find it, searched for its fresh and cold, and they look like fools, having come so far to feel stupid.

That's how you let me down just now — and out of cowardice! You didn't need to fear.

Did I ask to borrow your money? Did I say: 'I've been kidnapped — ransom me!' or 'I've been captured by bandits — lead a troop to the rescue!'

You didn't need to prove my losses were just — I'm not asking you to defray them.

But if you *can* explain to me where I was wrong — I'm silent, go on and tell!

You just and moral men, so sure, such stern pronouncers of judgement — you've come to your smug indignant decision, and what does it prove?

Your speechifying's an argument — and the words of a man in despair are just wind?

The Unholy Bible

Unbending men, so exactingly just you'd auction off an orphan or sell a friend to collect an overdue debt,

do me a favor and look me in the eye, tell me to my face I'm a liar.

If you didn't need so bad to be the ones in the right you'd see I'm not in the wrong.

Don't you think I'd know the taste of a lie on my tongue, admit it and spit it away?

(7)

Isn't life on earth like a military term of service, one long day's labor for little pay?

You wait for night and labor's end like a panting sweating slave, like a hired man watching the clock till he can go home with his wage.

But the time I've been given to serve is worse — my months a cheating measure of moons: night, which offers all their inheritance of rest, only doles and draws out my woe.

I lie down already wishing it was day, night extends me an unending portion of exhausted tossing till dawn.

Dirt-caked rags cover my skin — itself a cracked and oozing piece of hide.

My days flicker past faster than a weaver's shuttle. They brought no hope. They'll not be back.

Did you forget my life's a moment, a breath? — if I don't see happiness with these eyes I'm never going to.

Nor will you see me again in some aftertime — if you turn away now, by the time you look back I'll be gone.

Man dissolves like a cloud, fades traceless into Sheol,

he never finds his way back home, the places he was known forget he ever was.

And I won't be quiet — you sure weren't — I hurt and

Job

I'm going to talk, let my pain think out loud.

Do I roar ocean-loud? Spout blasphemy like a whale's blow-hole? that you stand there like a lighthouse to warn others away?

All I wanted was to bed down and forget, the covers pulled over my head,

but you come here and terrorize me with your nightmare visions and gods in the dark.

All I want now is extinction — to cease being me and just not be.

I wouldn't even want to live forever! And seeing my whole life's three heart-beats long, so short I scarcely even exist — can't you leave me alone?

Jah, what is man — you make such a fuss over him — why pay him any attention?

You test him every instant, find new faults in him each day —

how long are you going to stare at me? won't you let up for a second, let me swallow my spit in peace?

Even if I *had* sinned, how does that effect you, always watching mankind like a cop? why'd you set me up to be your target and nothing but a burden to myself?

Why won't you forgive, lift the weight of blame?

Now I sit in the dirt. Soon I'll be under it, and not even you will find me again.

(8)

Bildad answered:

How long are you going to gust and squall this kind of haughty talk?

Does God judge wrong or decide for a lie?

Obviously your kids sinned and God saw to it their crimes caught up with them;

obviously, if you ask mercy and show yourself eager for God

The Unholy Bible

and if you're really pure and upright, he'll jump to help you this minute and restore you what your righteousness earned, all you had will look little to the much you'll get.

Don't believe me? Examine what the ancients taught, you may accept our forefathers' findings —

hey, what can we know? we were born this morning, what could we have learned in a life as long as our shadow and faster in the passing?

Let the old wisdom teach you, listen to it make its points.

Can papyrus plants rise except when there's swamp, or reeds grow where there's no water?

No, their shoots, even untouched, unplucked, are the first grass to dry and die if they can't soak their roots.

And that's the way things succeed for those who forget about God — just when success has them hoping big things it's all destroyed.

Their plans hang from a frailer thread than a spider would trust her weight on.

They've floored their house with rotten wood, the roof creaks ominous overhead.

They're like a plant that shows fresh and green in early spring, sending out shoots to the ground around it,

but its tendrils only wind around rock, gropingly grow over stones, meet no moist dirt —

when the heavy suns come it's gone, dried up, blown off, not a root remains.

That's the quick joy of the Godless life — an hour's thriving, and another grows where he was.

But God doesn't abandon the innocent or put power in wicked men's hands.

He'll have you laughing out loud again — and right in your enemies' faces.

Then they'll be the ones humiliated, homeless and alone.

Job

(9)

Job answered:

I agree, God only punishes the wicked —

since his definition of wicked has nothing to do with actual guilt.

If you're innocent and try to defend yourself, he doesn't listen to one word in a thousand,

no matter how smart or strong you are, you get no benefit from strictly stating the clearest case —

no fact stands obstacle to the whim and will of God.

If a mountain's in his way, in a second it's someplace else, and as if there always, not a grass-blade out of place.

His snort of impatience could send the earth skittering out of orbit,

at his "No" the sun doesn't rise and the frighted stars hide under night.

He's the one who pitched the sky's blue tent, he tramps across the ocean on the backs of tidal waves,

he arranged the constellations, from the Great Bear and Orion in the north, down through the Pleiades and all the southern stars.

He makes more wonders than you could count even if you were wise enough to recognize them all.

He could be here now and I not know it, pass enormously on unremarked.

No one can keep him from seizing whatsoever — who could demand an explanation from Him?

He never revokes what he's wrought in wrath. Chaos is still cringing from when he beat her into the shapes of the created.

Can you really think I'm going to answer him back, even try to communicate?

The Unholy Bible

Supposing I don't upbraid him with my innocence, just beg him to judge me with mercy,

— if I cry out to God and he answers, I don't trust it'll be because he really listened and was touched.

His reply will be to flick me off the ground with a hurricane and smash me back to earth, without cause, and for sure without a word.

Before I could take a breath after my first words he'd give me pain enough to shut me up.

If it's a question of power, he'll answer any man, but for justice — what court do we summon him to?

So I'm in the right — he can torture confessions from me, make me rename purity sin.

But I am blameless here — I don't care if I die for saying it — it's true. So kill me! I spit on my life.

I say: it's all one — guilty, innocent, God executes both alike.

God laughs when sinless people are shot down on an instant's whim.

Earth belongs to the strong and evil. God blinds all judges, there's no appeal. If this isn't God's work, whose is it?

My time on earth runs, gone and brought no good,

faster than a light ship before a heavy wind, than an eagle zooming earthwards after prey.

I tell myself "Stop pondering the pain. Look up again, relearn how to smile."

But I can't. Dread soaked into my bones. I don't trust God will ever acquit or forgive.

To him I remain a man condemned. Why struggle for a change that can't come?

If I washed in water from whitest snow, scrubbed my hands with raw lye,

in his eyes I'd still be fresh-dredged from the pigsty, so

Job

filthy my own clothes try to slip off out of loathing.

How expect he'd relent? he's not a man so you could reason and respond, you can't go with him before an impartial judge,

no one could lay a hand on both our shoulders and mediate between us, make him put down the whip so he can't make me cower and squeak.

If that could be, I'd speak out unafraid — but that's not how it stands.

(10)

I'm disgusted I still live. I'm going to abandon all thoughtful caution, let the pain talk.

I say to God: don't just condemn me! tell me what your charges against me are.

Do you like to bully and beat? do you enjoy throwing away a being you constructed and pouring sunshine on whatever the wicked want?

You made the human eye — can you look through it, see things from a human point of view?

When it comes to seeking out my faults and hunting for my sins you're as urgent as if you'd only a man's span, the brief chance of the creature that counts its life in years, — despite the fact you know I'm not guilty! You take your unfair aim in full knowledge I can't escape it.

Your hands formed, assembled me — now you swallow me up into nothing?

Remember! I'm just a thing you made from clay, one you'll return to dirt.

Didn't you spurt me into existence like milk from a teat? make me take shape like curds, harden like cheese,

didn't you congeal me into soft fetal bones woven over in thinnest muscle, wrapped in translucent flesh?

The Unholy Bible

You showed me such kindness — you showed me life!
Your infinite attentions protected my breaths
   — and all the time you were treasuring up *this* fate for me?
Yes, you, the architect of all that occurs.

You just waited for me to sin — and destroyed me for it.
If I'm innocent, so what? I'm too sated with humiliating pain
to so much as raise my head.

If I stood up you'd pounce on me like a lion and teach me
better than to pray at you — you'll hurl my words right back,

redouble your judgements against me, irritate your own
anger, send in fresh troops.

Why did you ever bring me out of the womb? I could have
just died in its darkness.

I'd have been as if I'd never been, carried straight from the
belly to the grave.

Won't I leave off being in a little anyway? Can't you ease
up for that brief, let my last days brighten?

before I go the path I won't travel back, Death's Black-
land, Shadow-Valley,

where there's only light enough to see how dark it is, Mot
the Death-god's non-realm, where dawn is a gloom seeping
black from the horizon, the reversed and Chaos kingdom
where night is day.

(11)

Zophar answered:

Should sheer mass of words outweigh any answer? Will
we be jabbered into agreeing he's right?

You ramble on and we sit dumb; mock us, we don't dare
talk back and put you in your place.

You call out to God: "I know full well I'm innocent —
what's more, you know it too!"

Job

Is no one willing to take God's side and match words with you?

to impart to you the mysterious wisdom that no one-sided argument is true,

and here the other side is: however God punishes man, it's less than he deserves.

Have you really fathomed the mind of God? you know his limitations?

Those limits are the limitless heights of sky — how do you deal with that? They're more unsearchably deep than Sheol — how far can you peer towards the bottom of that blackness?

They're broader than earth, wider than sea.

He lets pass or recaptures or gathers together whatever he pleases — who's to stop him?

— and why should they try? he knows who's guilty — don't you think he recognizes sin when he sees it?

Though Man's an empty-headed kind of creature, he should try to wise up and wake up — even though he's born to be jackass stubborn.

Now if you'd get control of your own mind, calm down and stretch out suppliant arms to God,

throw away whatever sin you're holding on to, don't protect it like your house-guest,

then you could look up to God with clear-eyed blameless face, stand fearless, firm as a man cast in iron,

you'd forget your pain like last year's rain,

your life would brighten clear as afternoon, fresh as morning light,

you'd recover your trust because there *would* be hope, the closest look around would show you all secure, you'd go again easy to sleep.

People would look at you with their old respect, the eyes of your enemies avoid your glance,

The Unholy Bible

they'd have no cover or excuse for their malice — their ill-wishes for you would die with a gasp.

(12)

Job answered:

Well now the entire assembly has passed its unanimous judgement, the concentrated wisdom of the whole people — when you three die wisdom leaves the race of men.

But I've got a brain too, and no worse than yours. Who couldn't come up with this level of insight, these false and easy explanations of my case?

I'm a laughing-stock to my friends — as far as you can see I'm still asking God long after he's given his answer. The fact that I'm innocent and upright is nothing but a subject for jeers.

Misfortune always seems earned, deserving a sneer, in the minds of people sitting secure, safe beside catastrophe.

And everything's tranquil in the homes of real criminals, all's easy for those who provoke God, they still hold what-. ever he's given them.

Don't listen to me — ask the animals — they'll teach you, the birds in the sky — they'll tell,

the very plants in the ground know the story, the ocean's fish will speak it and leave nothing out,

not one among these but knows anything that happens is an act of God's deliberate will, in his hand the life of every creature, and the breath of all who wear human flesh — but they have no illusions about that hand's being *fair*.

Isn't the ear supposed to test words like the tongue tastes food?

Isn't age supposed to have experience, don't many days lived make for wisdom? Then why don't you understand?

Well God has all knowledge, all strength, and he knows full well what he does,

Job

he tears down with no intention of rebuilding, traps a man and never lets him go,

he shuts off the springs, lets rivers run dry, or sends them in torrents to wash away the land,

he's the giver of power and insight, and he makes one man mislead so another man errs,

he makes wise councilors be lead off barefoot captives, degrades ministers of state into slaves,

he takes away a king's judgment and self-restraint so he ruins the realm for a tight skirt,

God has even priests auctioned off as chattel, wipes out their inherited dignities,

he twists the words of trusted advisors, takes away prudent elders' common sense,

he drowns princes in shame, opens holes in a warrior's armor,

he pulls secrets out of their darkness, makes clear day black and baffling as death,

he raises high a people then annihilates them, scatters them among nations then leads them back,

he confuses their leaders, makes them wander at random, knowing no road,

they grope their way as if in the dark, reel and stagger like drunks.

(13)

My eyes have seen, my ears have heard, I've understood this thing.

I'm no less able than you to figure it out.

Even so, I still want to try words with the Almighty, to bring my case before El,

— but you, you lie to me about God's nature — and not even comforting lies!

The Unholy Bible

If only you'd just shut up — then you could at least look wise.

I'm only asking you to listen to my defense, try and grasp the basis of my plea.

How can you be so dishonest with God, lying to him about him to his face?

Do you think you you'll flatter your way out when God is sitting in judgement?

Do you think false fawning and fat praises will work when he explores your heart? Do you think you'll cheat God like he was a man and then go laugh it off?

Have you no fear of his majesty? Can't you feel the terror of God?

Before him your wise sayings won't stand up any better than scribblings in the dust when the storm wind drives, all your defenses — sand-castles.

Hold back your indignant answers, let me speak, come upon me for it what may.

Why should I bite my lip and say nothing, hug myself to clamp back the words?

Let him kill me — I hope for no better — I stand right in front of him reading out my unstained record,

and he'll *have* to rescue me, because no sinner *can* stand before him — *therefore* he must become witness to my innocence.

Listen carefully, carefully, let your ears take in my statement:

I've set my case in order, double-checked it, I know I'll be shown right.

Who can prove otherwise? speak now, I'll shut up and quietly die.

God, I offer myself naked, unflinching, to your decision — but on these two conditions:

Job

don't strike me down with your fist as I speak or shake me with your terrors.

You ask the questions, I'll answer; or I'll tell while you listen to me.

Let me know what and how many are my crimes, sins and faults.

Why do you hide your presence from me as if I were your enemy?

Why crush a papery wind-driven leaf? why root out and destroy me whom am no more than dry stubble?

Have you sourly recorded and learned by rote all the stupid things I did as a boy?

You caught me! I'm human, I stand convicted of being a fallible creature of flesh —

disease-rotted flesh at that, worn to holes like a motheaten coat.

(14)

We humans, children of Woman, have only a narrow measure of life and that brim-filled with fears,

we bloom and wither fast as a flower, we last like shadows running from the sun.

On *this* you turn your all-searching eye? *I'm* worth summoning before you in judgement?

Who could expect perfect purity in a creature shaped from dirt? No one!

Haven't you already unchangeably engraved my sum of days, numbered every month, set life before me like a task — only so far then finish?

then lighten your hand pressing heavy upon me, let your servant take what pleasure he can in his given work.

There's hope for a cut-down tree, it may yet send up new leaf and shoot,

The Unholy Bible

though its ancient roots are dry as rock in the sod and its trunk sticks up dead from the dirt,

at the mere scent of water it musters a sprout, blossoms up sudden as a sapling would,

but a man once dead is felled for good — when his body dies, what's left?

for him, poor plant, the sea might as well be dry, and every river parched to a runnel of dust — this tree no water restores.

A man's laid out, he will not rise. There'll cease to be a sky before he starts up and wakes from the grave-deep sleep.

If only you buried me in Sheol like treasure, planning to dig up and recover me, if only you just hid me there till your wrath were past —

then, at a set time, remembered me again.

If a dead man lived again — then I'd wait hopeful through my whole term of service for the time I'd be relieved,

when you'd feel a longing for this creature you built, when you'd call my name — and I'd answer!

But now you count against me my every step, don't even wait for me to sin.

You've rolled up tight the scroll that records my faults, sealed it with a smear of slander and stamped that like clay with the signet of untruth.

Even the mountains finally wear down level with the plain, their great rock masses shift and subside,

ceaseless water wears out stone, rains gnaw away the earth,

and human hope, more enduring than these, that too you finally destroy.

Batter forever at a man, he turns away; age reshapes, sorrow lengthens his face, he gives up.

His children get success — it doesn't register. They go hungry, he doesn't recognize them, can't care,

Job

nothing's left of him but a pulse and pain and a great vague memory of grief.

(15)

Eliphaz answered:

Does an intelligent man respond to words senseless as the roaring of the wind? If he opens his mouth to speak all he gets is a lungful of the hot air blowing in his face.

Why engage an argument going nowhere? You can't fill an empty premise with sense.

But your statements demand response — because they undermine reverent dread of God, shear away religious devotion,

because your tongue persuades to your style of sin, your lips teach a reasoned, clever wickedness.

It's not me but your own words that condemn you, your own mouth provides evidence and answer.

Are you the firstborn of mankind, the primordial person, older than earth, formed before the hills?

Did you hear God's secret plans for the creation? did you take such a share of the original wisdom as diminished the remaining stock?

What do you know that we don't? What do you understand that we can't?

We're white-haired elder men, greater in days than your father!

Is all God's compassion too little for you, do you call his gentleness neglect?

Your mind is working backwards, you dream with open eyes when you set your inspiration against God and breathe out this kind of talk.

You ask: "What is Man that he's expected to be flawless,

81

The Unholy Bible

how can the child of Woman be perfectly just?"

You're right about that — God can't even trust the angels, the clear skies don't look pure enough to him.

Of course Man goes wrong, becomes corrupt — he absorbs error naturally, with no plan to — necessarily, just as he drinks water.

I'm talking now, so you listen to me. I know you don't care for my visions, but I saw this too and I'm going to describe it,

the same as the ancient sages related, an unhidden wisdom since the time of *their* ancestors,

of the earliest men to be born in this land, before they even knew other peoples existed.

That first folk saw that the wicked man writhes in anxiety every day, through the whole sum of years set aside for his goodly portion.

He hears his worst fear in every sound, and when he finally calms down, that's when his destroyer comes.

And when the shadow falls on him he knows he can't out-run the one who casts it — they're waiting for him, swords out and well sharpened.

When he's on the run and hungry, who's going to give him bread? He knows at any instant his day could go death-black.

He shivers, knowing he's trapped. Terror stands before him like an armored king about to lead the attack.

And this is the man who dared oppose God, who bragged like a soldier, the hero who didn't fear all-powerful Jah,

who set himself against God, lowered head and bull-charged, trusting his thick shield against every missile.

Conqueror-calm, he looked out through the slitty eyes in his fat face, sat solid and confident, his blubber hanging heavy over his crotch,

secure in his citadels — about to be destroyed, his houses — about to burn, every structure ready to become rubble.

Job

Judge how rich he is, how long his wealth will last, how far his holdings overspread earth —

he can't escape his doom any more than he could outrun nightfall, death eats his offspring with him, they go like green leaves ash-whitening on a tree in flames, he and his family name end with his breath.

Let no man trust and get giddy over cheating schemes — what he recieves in the end will rob him worst.

Before his measure of life plays out, beforethe tree of his Being greens full foliage,

God tears him away like you'd pluck an unripe grape or rip off an olive tree's early blossom.

A sinner's family ends with him, sterile, gone with its name; fire inherits the tents of bribe-takers.

His life's work is a false pregnancy, labor and pains that bring to light their own lie, a belly bloated with air, a wombful of nothing.

(16)

Job answered:

I've heard so much like this I know it by rote. Your counselings are as bad as the suffering itself.

Will you go on restless, endless as the wind? What is it excites you to keep answering back?

If you were in my place, I wouldn't have trouble preaching either,

but I'd fascinate you with soothing words, nod my head, sympathetic, agreeing,

and utter such as shores up courage, the wish to comfort would govern my tongue.

Speaking puts no pause to my pain — if I'm silent and resigned, nothing changes,

either wearies me now.

83

The Unholy Bible

God, you've horrified all my friends,
you've shrivelled me into a scary portent, a symbol of your
wrath. My skinny limbs witness against me — I look as bad as
if I deserved this.

God-rage has torn me. He hates me so much he grinds
his teeth.

My enemy, his eyes beam evilly at me.

People come and gape at me, they're all ganged up against
me. Outraged, they smack my face;

God abandoned me to the power of the cruel, the evil own
me now.

I was all calm and cozy when God snapped me in pieces,
grabbed me by the neck, smashed me against the wall,
then propped me up as a target.

His army stands around me in a circle, skewering my heart
with their spears. I kneel in bloody mud.

God tackles me like an armored warrior, his impact redly
rends, widens wounds into one.

I wrap rags around my battered hide, lie with my face in
the dirt.

I cry so much my cheeks fiercely tingle, when I shut my
eyes I see a black foretaste of death.

And there's no stain on my innocent hands! blameless, I
continue to pray to him.

Earth, don't drink, don't hide my blood; sky, don't absorb
but forever re-echo my cry!

I shout my protest through the heavens, make him on high
my witness.

While my friends mock, my eyes trickle with longing for God.

If only I could argue with God as with a man, as a human
talks to his fellow,

— but already my life's short enough to count in hours,
I'm on the unreturning path.

Job

(17)

My breath would have drained away, my light been snuffed, I'd be looking up from the grave-pit

if my friends didn't taunt me forward into life, if they didn't quarrel my attention back to this existence.

God, give some surety you'll fairly handle my case! Ah, who's to shake my hand on such a promise?

Not these whose minds you've hidden from insight, you can't set *them* as judges over this.

These conscienceless flatterers have so far forgot what truth is that even their children will be morally blind.

You set me before all peoples as an object lesson. Edified, they spit in my face.

My eyes glaze over from frustration and rage. I feel like I'm vanishing into my own shadow, staggering back into blackness.

All righteous people are shocked by my case, the innocent say, startled, "Oh what a big sinner!

Good thing *I'm* on the path of the pure!" Everyone feels encouraged and justified.

Why don't you all just leave? I'm not going to applaud your discernment.

My time is gone, my plans cut off, I comprehend no more.

I can't see the difference between day and night — to me it's all night now.

If I have any hope or home now it's Sheol — to pull its shadow over me like a blanket and sleep.

Death is my family, the Grave is my father, the Maggot my mother and sister.

Where have you gone, my hopes? to what remote land was your flight, what traveller saw you passing?

I drag my legs down the steps to Sheol and pray that that's the end.

The Unholy Bible

(18)

Bildad answered:

How long must we go on mending a net of argument he just keeps tearing through? Let's reflect and then pronounce.

Why should we be left staring, big-eyed and wordless as cows?

He's insane — he's ripping apart his soul.

Job, do you really think you're proof that the Rock which supports all being's been pulled out from under, that God's deserted the earth?

The light of the wicked will be put out, his flame can't flicker bright for long,

his tent goes dark, his candle blown.

His wealth only hobbles him now, he stumbles over his own bad plans

and right into the net spread for his steps, he's put his foot in the trap,

the noose pulls tight around his ankle, and that strong rope will hold.

It was hidden, that snare, in the ground he walked; not visible, yet right in the middle of his road,

and now he flinches for fear all around, scrambling in panic.

Now all his having's become hunger and want, disaster waits ready for his fall.

Disease, the firstborn son of Death, eats his skin by bits, then grabs whole limbs.

Dragged out of his house and safety, he's sent packing to Death, the King of Terrors.

Death moves into his empty tent, tills his fields, sowing brimstone to make them forever sterile.

That man's roots dry dead in the dirt, his leafage crisps and withers above.

Job

His very memory passes from the land. No one in the towns has even heard of his family.

He's thrown out of light into darkness, evicted from existence.

He has no children left, no kin among the people, no survivors where he lived.

The young are stunned by the judgement passed upon him; the old, who've seen so much, shiver seeing this.

These then are the wealthy dwellings of the wicked, the choice place and estate of those who don't recognize God.

(19)

Job answered:

How long will you go on saddening my soul, hurting me with words?

Ten times now you've tried to humiliate me — doesn't any shame restrain you from gouging a man who's down?

Suppose I really have gone wrong — the madness and mistake are mine — not yours.

If you're resolved to set yourselves up superior, upbraiding, disgracing me in high moral tone —

then don't forget you're blaming God too — if I sinned it was unawares, tricked into it, trapped by God — he made me stray, he threw the invisible net I struggle under.

I cry: "Help!" but get no answer, howl for justice that doesn't come.

He walls me in with ignorance — if I don't know what I did, how can I leave the sin? He's laid such darkness on my path I can't see where I am.

He stripped people's respect from me, honor's been taken from my head easy as knocking off a hat.

Whichever way I turn, he pummels and I run. He tore out my hope like a sapling.

The Unholy Bible

His anger flames in my face. He thinks I'm his enemy.

His attacks come at me all at once, an army; they trench in, heap siegeworks, encamp around my tent.

My brothers watch from a distance, my friends just look away.

Neighbors, acquaintances — I don't see them any more. Men who were my guests don't remember my name,

my slave-girls treat me like a foreigner, an unknown from far away.

I call for my slaves — none come, not even if I beg.

My wife is disgusted I'm still alive; you can imagine what a pleaser I am to my kids —

even the young ones despise me — if I so much as raise my head they shout "Shut him up!"

Men I talked, shared plans with, loathe me. Friends I loved and love — *they've* changed.

My bones stick out, they tent my skin. I've escaped with nothing but the teeth in my head.

Have mercy, pity me, you, my friends — I've been touched by the hand of God.

Why do you persecute me like God, clawing for my mind, not content with my flesh?

If only my words were written down, inscribed in the pages of a book,

writ with iron pen, cut into sheets of lead, hewn forever into stone!

I'd know I had a living witness, lasting past, standing up for me on earth,

so when this body wrecks and rots I could, with my words, still stare back accusingly at God —

if only I could confront him myself, with my own and actual eyes!

my gut is sick with wishing this.

Job

But you, my friends, keep saying: "Come on, we almost have him. We really know his problem to its root."

Be afraid, be death-afraid, what you're doing's a death-deserving crime,

and you may learn there really *is* a judge.

(20)

Zophar answered:

The thought that might be so holds me back and flusters me.

I hear the rebuke — it almost shames me — but my understanding tells me: "No. Go ahead!"

Don't you know, Job, that since forever, since Man was first put on earth,

the joy of the wicked's always almost over, a sinner's glad for an instant?

Though rank and position make him think he's a god looking down through the clouds,

he's obliterated like shit on the ground, gone so fast no one knows where,

flown like a dream — who can find him? like the phantom world of sleep that flutters off when you wake.

The eye saw him — but no more. His home never glimpses him again.

His sons, ashamed of his wealth, scatter it to charity.

He was still strong as a younger man — that strength is buried with him.

Evil was sweet as candy to him, he cherished it under his tongue,

he sucked on it slow to make it last, gently tongued it up against his palate,

but that sweet suck turned in his belly, it's rattlesnake venom inside him.

89

The Unholy Bible

He swallowed down wealth — now he'll vomit it up. God pummels his stomach till he pukes.

He suckled viper venom — the poison spreads from his center.

He thought he'd float forever on tides of wealth, skimming the cream off a wave of luxury;

he sweated for it — now he has to give it back untasted, he never gets to crow from the top of his gold-heap.

He crushed the poor and left them lying; built no home, only robbed one;

no matter how fat his belly never felt full, and his greed left nothing over,

he ate it all, put nothing by; then it was all good for Now: now it's all back then for good.

With far more than enough he still itched for more, felt poverty always just behind him, about to tap his shoulder.

Just when he was lolling gorged, God's anger sprayed him with flame, seared him at his table: a blackened man at a dish full of cinders.

He fled at the sight of God's iron-tipped arrows, but the bow of brass shot them right through him.

He draws one out of his belly, sees the point pull glinting from his ruptured gut — and comprehends terror.

His treasure-house becomes his tomb. He fries in a fire no human could have lit — spitted on a lightning bolt. And it goes no better with those left in his tent.

The sky sheds light on his crimes, earth covers none of them.

All his goods spew out from his house, broadcast in judging God's anger-day.

That's the wicked man's God-given heritage, his promised portion from El.

Job

(21)

Job answered:

Listen, listen to my words, and take comfort in this coming repayment of your patience:

endure it that I speak, and afterwards

you'll get to ridicule my thoughts.

Why shouldn't I be frustrated? it's not a man but God I'm asking for fairness.

Turn, look at me, be stunned! Gape, put your hands to your mouth!

As often as I remember what's happened I start shaking, terror encompasses me like my own body.

Why is it that the wicked, unlike me, live, get old still strong, noble, rich and happy?

They see their children, then their grandchildren, safe, living with them.

God never strikes their peaceful, fearless homes.

Their pregnant cattle never miscarry, their cows deliver frequent and easy,

their families extend quick as their herds, their children frisk and gambol strong as calves,

they make joy-noise with drum and flute and harp,

their days slip by in happiness — when they die, it's an instant's terror, no more,

they tell God: "Go somewhere else, don't be bothering us! We don't want to know about your rules.

Who's the Almighty that we should serve him? What do we stand to gain from going to him?"

Their own and godless efforts made *them* happy — but me, I chose a different plan!

Now how can you say the wicked's lamp will be put out, that their misery's on the way?

The Unholy Bible

that an angry God will assign them pain?

that they're about to be scattered like straw in the wind, chaff snatched by the storm?

You'll counter: "God's saving up his punishment to visit on their children, they'll all yet pay in full and know what it's for. The wicked live on — to see a greater disaster, they'll drink the full cup of almighty wrath. What pleasure can they finally have in their holdings when all their months are numbered?"

Do you realize you're teaching God, the judge on high, the way he *ought* to act?

One man dies, still strong, uninjured, the calm end of a quiet life,

muscles firm, forehead smooth, blood rich from feeding well;

another dies, embittered to the soul, he never tasted the good things of this world.

There's no fairness in their different portions, it's no justice that they lie in the same earth, equally worm-food in the end.

Oh, I understand the way you think — your rationalizations rend me, they're oppression to all who suffer.

You ask: "Where now's the house of the wealthy and wicked?"

Why don't you ask passers-by at random, maybe you'll believe what every one of them knows, their plain talk's an oracle even you can interpret.

Are the evil spared for some day of judgement? led insensibly to where fury will explode over them?

Who's going to tell those wretched sinners to their face where they're heading? Who's going to make them pay for what they've done?

When they finally *are* led to the cemetery, it's in pomp and solemn cortege, an honor-watch is posted at the graveside.

Sweet lies the sod on the evil dead — since everyone marches

Job

in the funeral procession, led by numberless notable men.

What nothing you comfort me with! Your answers are shown up for cheating lies.

(22)

Eliphaz answered:

Do you think when a man is prudent he's doing God a favor?

Do you think God waits eager for you to be just? That God owes you something, that he makes an unfair profit if your doings are pure?

Or do you think he's prosecuting you on account of your incredible reverence?

Aren't you actually enormously wicked and limitlessly sinful?

Don't you exploit your own brothers, extort the shirt off a naked man?

You wouldn't offer water to one fainting from thirst, you'd refuse a starving man bread.

You're powerful — the earth is yours — the people bow down before you!

You turn away widows empty-handed, you break an orphan's arms!

That's why you're afraid of everything now, the cause of your terror out of nowhere,

of this dark confusion you can't see through, the death-dread flooding you under.

Isn't God above, like the sky, dominating all? See the stars in their height and infer how supreme is He!

But you say: "Does El even know what happens here below? He can't see down through his own clouds to judge,

sequestered in the upper sky's gauzy fog-banks, he doesn't watch us but only strolls around the circuit of that uppermost blue."

The Unholy Bible

Will you keep forever to that old same road walked by every evil man before you?

Do you want, like them, an early death, that you build your house-foundations on rushing waters? like those who tell God: "Get away from us!" Well, what do you think the Almighty's going to do to them?

God fills their homes with wealth? I want no share of it on their terms:

let the just man just watch — he'll be glad at what he sees. The innocent will laugh at *them* in the end.

All their wealth will vanish, translated into flames.

Accept and yield to God and it'll be well with you. You've everything to gain if you do these things:

recieve his teachings, try to understand his words.

Kick your sins right out of your house, come back to God, he'll build you up again.

Shake off all regret for the gold you lost just like you'd brush off dust, throw away your remembered gems like pebbles into a stream.

Make the Almighty your treasure, hold God as your over-stuffed wallet,

because when you look up to God and find in him your delight,

and pray to him — he'll hear you! next you'll be offering sacrifices of thanks,

whatever you plan will come to pass, you'll be walking in the light.

When men knock you down you'll call it a promotion, so clear you'll know God saves the humbled heart-broke man.

If you're innocent, he'll rescue; you're saved insofar as you're pure.

Job

(23)

Job answered:

Still new bitter considerings eat into my brain. I'm so weak from long groaning pain my hand feels too heavy to raise.

If only I knew where to find him! I'd come to him where he lives,

I'd set my case before him — my mind is full of what I'd say.

Oh to make my statements and have him answer, to find out how he'd reply!

Would he shut me up by a show of force? But no, he'd listen to me.

Were there a chance an upright man could argue his case with him — I'd make him acquit me forever.

I walk forward searching for God, go back, he isn't there either.

I see his actions all around me, but him I can't grasp — he causes and disappears.

But he knows my life's whole road. Every test he put me to, I emerged pure as gold from the furnace,

I marched hard in his footsteps, eyes always on his path and never turned aside.

I didn't disregard a one of his commandments, treasured in my heart every word of his law —

but he's independent of all, complete, aloof — no one can turn him — whatever he wishes he ineluctably does,

he executes his decrees in full — what he's begun to do to me he will much more,

that's why I dread him, this is the reflection that puts me in terror of God,

this makes my trapped heart thud:

that he *hasn't yet* killed me — what a darkening then awaits me before he brings on night!

The Unholy Bible

(24)

Why doesn't the Almighty set aside a time of judgement, why don't those who strive to know him ever see his reckoning-day?

Men move the boundary stones, grabbing others' land, keep for themselves the herds pastured there as well,

they lead off the orphan's sole inheritance — a mule, take a widow's one ox as interest on a debt.

The poor wander out in the wasteland, looking for a place to hide their dispossessed selves.

Look, the wild ass in the desert's free to feed on what's there, to pursue its grassy affairs,

cropping all the fodder earth and generous nature offer them and their young each day,

they stray and graze at the plowed lands of men, they browse the leaves of the rich man's vineyard,

but the human poor sleep naked, not even a blanket against the cold,

houseless, crouched in hill-caves, hugging the rock for cover, soaked by every rain.

The wicked rich tax and exact, enslave as payment the baby at the breast,

while the poor walk without even a shirt, the starving shoulder the rich man's bushels,

the hungry harvest him his olives, the thirsty press his wine.

From the cities rise the groans of the poor like cries of the wounded on a battlefield,

and God doesn't see how insane this all is.

These things are done defiantly, in daylight, men ignore God's ways as though he'd never shown them,

Job

they wake up in the morning ready to kill, all day long they slaughter the wretched and poor.

In daylight they do this — at least the petty thief has enough shame to do his work by night,

even the adulterer, impatient, waits for twilight, taking care he's unseen, ashamed to show his face and have it known.

Burglars break in under darkness — in daylight they're indoors asleep, they don't even see much less outface day,

in daylight they'd be killed, dawn would be their doomsday, if they don't fear God at least they do Death.

Oh God, you who move invisible and quick as the wind across the sea,

will you never move against the rich, curse their heriting the earth, their lifelong leisured stroll through its vineyards?

May Sheol eat them for their sins as the sun in a drought would devour snow.

Feed them to grave worms! Be they forgot even by their own mothers,

crack their evil power like a sapling!

May the herds in their pastures be barren and do their widows no good,

though they employ private armies let them wake at midnight in terror for their lives,

when all's secure and calm let them fear the whispers of those they pay to protect them,

let these leaders of men disappear suddenly, let them sink with all they've amassed

easy as snapping dead a stalk of grain.

If this isn't how things should be — and are not — tell me I'm a liar. But you can't deny a word.

The Unholy Bible

(25)

Bildad answered:

God rules, God is frightening, he who calms the storming sky.

Is there any number to his powers? who doesn't his light reach?

How can a man seem just before God? The child of Woman, how could he be pure?

Even the moon shows stains, its brightness no cause for boasting, starlight itself doesn't seem perfectly clean to Him.

How then a Human, that worm of sixty winters? Man, that maggot on its way to the grave?

(26)

Job answered:

What strength have you offered the exhausted? what rescue have you brought to a man too weakened to lift his own arms?

How have you advised the man who's at a loss? what great sustaining insight have you given?

Have you thought at all about the person you hurl words at? Do you perceive how harsh a spirit breathes through your speeches?

The dead souls writhe and struggle to hide in Sheol's blackwater undersea world —

but the Pit is naked under God's gaze, the Abyss can hide nothing of what it's swallowed.

God sends the winds coursing wide and free through bare and hollow sky, suspends the earth in mid-nothing, resting on emptiness,

he binds up floods in his clouds, those vapory gates are enough to hold them back, they don't split under all that water's weight,

Job

he extends the levitating white prairies of cloud on which his throne sits sure,

he decreed the horizons and the dome of sky, regulating all its rainfall for as far a light and darkness reach,

North, South, East and West, the four frighted pillars of heaven, quake at his amazing thunder-shout,

terrified sea stampedes beneath; Rahab, the defiant, the violent, Rahab, Chaos-dragon of the waves, who surf-roars angry wordless noise — God gigantically whacks her and then by his insight tames her waters into orderly tides.

This done, God sighs — and the sky gentles bright and sweetly clear, while Rahab, that great water-snake, smit and fearing the fist, slides her apprehensive coils into hiding on ocean floor

— all this doesn't touch on the fringe of God's robe — it's just what whispery rumor of his being reaches us —

the full bomb-blast of his power, who can understand that language?

(27)

As God lives — he who's cheated me of justice and soured the soul inside me —

as long as the spirit lives in me, the live wind that is His breath keeps pumping through my lungs,

damned if I'll teach my tongue to lie or let my lips shape the deceits that would please you,

like Hell I'll wrongly call you right — till I die I'll not deny my own life's honest truth,

I'll hug my righteousness to me tighter, not even in thought will I slander my well-lived days.

Accuse me, attack me — go ahead — if anyone's wicked it's you —

The Unholy Bible

what good will you liars get to outweigh your loss of any
hope when God drags you up and examines your life?

Will God listen to your screams when suffering closes
over you?

Will God be all your delight even then? Will you ask him
to save you — from him?

I'll teach you what God has in store for you, what you'll
soon enough know,

all of you have seen it clear and true — never thinking it
applied to you —

this is what the wicked man gets from God, the inheritance
the violent grab from El:

if their children grow it's for sword-slaughter; their grandchildren won't see bread enough to fill their bellies ever,

Death eats their survivors, the widows don't even cry.

If gold coins rain on them numberless as dust-motes, if
their rich robes heap like snow-drifts,

it's the just who'll actually wear those wardrobes, the innocent who'll spend the silver.

Their homes are no surer than a moth's cocoon, frail as
the lean-to a field-watcher builds for a sun-shade.

They can fall asleep on a hill of gold — they'll wake up in
an empty room,

fear pulls them into its undertow, steals over them like a
hurricane's sudden darkness,

like a storm from the east Dread lifts and spins them, tor-
nado'd into the sky,

they scramble and grab in the hurling mid-air that has no
pity for their terror,

the storm thunderclaps its cloudy hands in glee and all
the winds whistle their derision.

Job

(28)

Man knows where to look for silver, the place to dig for gold,

he knows the smelting mysteries that make iron and bronze emerge from dirt,

he learns all things to their limit, pushing back the borders of whatever darkness hides, only Death is his boundary, the sole shadow he can't shine a light into,

he cuts canals, splits up rivers — where once water now roads and traffic flow;

he makes earth bristle grain for his bread.

Easy as stirring a fire to expose the glowing coals he turns up earth to show

the underground where sapphires lie common as rocks, the dirt that glitters gold ore.

Through mountains not even the eagle has seen, no vulture's eye has scanned,

not even the lions, those archetypes of pride who rove all rocky heights, not even they strode over such haughty hills —

there Man cuts roads through cliffs of solid flint, tears out by the roots any mountain in his way,

he turns rivers out of their deep rocky channels, exposing whatever treasure they covered:

their waters cut off to a weepy trickle, their secrets gleam out in daylight.

But Wisdom — where can Man find that? Where does Insight make its home?

No one even knows what it looks like — nothing else resembles it in the land of living men.

The Ocean says: "I don't have it, it isn't hiding in my depths."

The Unholy Bible

You couldn't buy Wisdom with a royal treasury, you can't weigh out its value in silver,

not with pure gold from Ophir, not with rare onyx or sapphire,

not with gold that's carefully worked, bowls, jars and plates in 24 carat.

Coral? Crystal? don't even think about it. A tear-drop of Wisdom's more than bushels of pearls,

you can't buy it with Ethiopian topaz, pure gold bars weigh nothing in the scales against insight.

Where does Wisdom come from? what place is Insight's home?

It's hidden from all that live, no bird's ever spied it from the sky.

Death and the Pit say: "We have heard certain rumors —

"God knows the roads that Wisdom travels, he's familiar with her home;

when he looked out to the limits of all underneath the sky

and established how much the weightless winds would weigh, the ends of the endless sea,

when he legislated the amount of rainfall, and resolved which way thunder would roll and lightning writhe,

when he looked to all this he saw Wisdom and made her his measure, set her up as a standard, explored her limits and her use,

and told Man: "As far as you're concerned,

to be in awe of God — that's wisdom, and insight consists in refusing to do wrong."

(29)

If only I could live again as once, when God watched over my days,

Job

and led me through my nights, his light shining down on me, a lamp,

when my life was in its harvest time, and God sat in my tent like a friend;

God was with me, and all around me — my children.

It seemed the streams ran milk for me, my olive-trees gushed oil;

when I went to join the council of elders at the city gate, I was given the wide seat of honor,

when they saw me, children hid, and rich men stood up to greet me,

princes broke off their conversation and put their finger to their lips,

merchants stopped their squabbles and stood like mutes,

every ear listened to me, and afterwards every tongue said "Good!" Every eye looked approval,

because if a poor man or an orphan without defender cried out, I rescued them,

slaves called down blessings on my head, I made widows laugh again,

I put on righteousness like a garment, and justice clothed itself in me: fairness made me look noble, not my turban or my robe.

I was eyes to the blind, legs for the cripple,

a father to the needy — taking on the cases of people I didn't even know.

I broke the teeth of wealthy sharks, made sure their prey escaped,

I thought I'd live as many years as there are grains of sand, like the Phoenix in its cassia and frankincense nest that only dies giving birth to itself,

I thought my roots would keep on drinking deep from underground streams and the morning dew ever refresh my fields,

The Unholy Bible

my power would always renew itself, the bow in my hand
stay supple as living wood.

People waited trembling for my advice, and listened, silent
and intent to understand,

after I spoke they wanted no other opinion, but just to let
my words sink in.

They'd stand silent, imploring my counsel, anxious as a
farmer in drought staring open-mouthed at the sky.

If I smiled at them, they couldn't believe it, their faces
brightened, taking light from mine.

I helped them choose their route, a leader; I comforted
the grieving like a king giving courage to his troops.

(30)

But now, they laugh at me, men lesser than me in age,

men whose fathers I wouldn't have trusted as much as the
dogs that watch my flocks,

men without the stamina for any respectable work,

beggars and outcasts, grown useless in hunger and
poverty, driven out of every settlement, who hide in the desert
and the waste,

who feed on whatever roots and berries they can pluck
from the scrub,

thieving nomads, chased from the towns with curses and
shouts,

who sleep in dry riverbeds, in holes, in the fissures of
rocks,

who live under bushes, who bray among the nettles like
wild asses,

men without religion, men without family, men afraid —
and rightly — to show themselves in any city.

Now I'm the hero of their taunting songs, their proverb is

Job

"worse off than Job,"

they despise me — even they avoid me — except to spit
in my face,

no bond of respect bridles them back, they look me in the
eye and hiss;

the mob comes up against me, they trip me with a kick, dig
a pit for me to fall in,

they shove me from the road, add force to my fall — they
need no help, it's easy enough.

They troop in at me as though through a breach in a city's
wall; they writhe on the ground, laughing at the wreck I am.

Terror rolls over me, chases me down the road like a wind,
all hope of rescue blown away like a cloud,

now my soul pours out with every groan, days of pain
have seized me,

pain bores through my bones, restlessly gnaws me at
night,

God's awful power is on me like a garment, its collar throt-
tles my neck,

he throws me into the mud — I lie there little better than
the dirt beneath me.

God! I cry out for your help — you don't answer; you only
notice when I try to stand up,

then you're present — as my enemy — I feel the hate in
your hands.

You hurl me onto the wind, make me ride the bucking
gusts — my brain melts from panic,

because I know you'll finally kill me like you do all that
lives.

No one I saved from their own disaster holds out a hand to
pull me from the rubble

though I wept when I heard of their hard times, my heart
went heavy for every wretch.

The Unholy Bible

I hoped for the best and recieved the worst, waited for day and only more night came,

and when day did come, it only brought my bowels more spasm and ache.

I shuffled along, bent over with grief, and no sun overhead; I stood up before the people, cried for help:

"I have no friend, no kin among you all — my only brothers are the jackals, my comrades are the ostrich's abandoned nestlings,

my skin is blackened from hunger, my bones burnt dry and white from thirst,

my harp plays dirges, out of tune and harsh, my flute sobs and keens."

(31)

When I was married, I swore an oath on my eyes — and kept it — I never even noticed another woman,

and what reward did God on high send down, what wage from towering Jah?

Wasn't it the wreck due a sinner, the ruin a criminal deserves?

Didn't he see all my goings? He counted my every step!

Did I walk the path of lies, did my legs carry me at a run towards deceit?

Let God weigh me in any fair scales, he'll see my purity.

If I turned from the right road, if I only looked and lusted, if my hands are stained by anything I touched,

I'll eat whatever I planted, roots and all!

If I was tempted by another woman, if I hid by her door waiting for the husband to leave,

may my wife grind grain as another's slave, may strangers get between her legs and pump.

Job

If I did such a crime, it requires the harshest judgement!

Adultery's a fire that eats a man's house down to its foundations, his fields down to their roots — if I committed it, let everything blaze!

If I wouldn't listen to my manservant or maidservant when they made complaint against me,

what could I hope for when God confronts me, how answer when he probes my heart?

Didn't he who made me make my slaves too? he gave us both shape in a woman's womb.

If I refused a poor man's request, if I made a widow cry,

if I ate my morsel all by myself and the orphan never shared it,

if I didn't rather raise him as if I were his father, and help him along as though we'd both one mother,

if I saw my worker without a shirt and didn't clothe his naked need,

if his shivering butt didn't bless me when the wool from my lambs covered him warm,

if I shook my fist and shouted at the little man because I knew I had power in court,

may my right arm break off at the shoulder and its forearm snap at the elbow!

But I feared God's punishment — at the thought of his power, I'd none to harm.

If I put my trust in gold, if I said to my coins: "I'm safe with you!"

If I rejoiced because I had wealth and exulted at owning so much,

if, when I saw the sun rise in brightness or the moon move in beauty,

I secretly raised my hands in prayer and greeted them as gods,

The Unholy Bible

— that would have been a crime to condemn me, it would show I'd forgotten God above.

If I was glad at the misfortune of a man who hated me, if I brayed with joy when bad befell him,

if I ever let my mouth so sin as to whisper the hope that he were dead;

if I didn't feed my servants so well they wished someone were hungry so the food wouldn't be wasted,

if my home wasn't open to the whole highway, if a traveller ever had to sleep out of doors,

if I ever sinned and hid it, buried it in my mind as people will and didn't confess it outright

through fear of what the crowd would think, scared of losing my status among the clans — if I kept it quiet and private;

if I did any of these things I wouldn't now hope for a hearing — but I never did! I take oath, affix my signature: now let the Almighty answer what I've said! My case couldn't be more clear and well-ordered if I'd written it out on a scroll

and held it up over my head for everyone to see.

I walk up to God, confident as a king, crowned with my just cause, ready to recount and account for every step I took.

If ever the land cried out because of me, if ever a tear fell in the furrows of its fields because of what I did,

if I got rich from it without paying well my workers, if I made my servants groan,

let it bring forth brambles, not wheat, for me, and in place of barley, weeds.

The speeches of Job were completed.[5]

(38)

And God answered Job from the midst of a hurricane:

Who's this polluting the intellectual air with uninformed opinion?

Job

Stand up like a man, buckle on your sword-belt: I'll ask, you answer to me!

Where were *you* when I laid the Earth's foundations? tell! if you know so much;

who took its measurements, surveyed its space — at least you must know *that*?

When the world's foundation stones were sunk in the void, what did they finally rest *on*? what holds them up in mid nothing? Who slid into place the keystone upholding the whole impossible arch

on that first of all mornings when the stars sang together and all the gods shouted with joy?

Who sealed off the ocean of Chaos, slammed a gate against it, put limits on its liquid infinity gushing from the womb of non-being?

who tamed the roaring blackness of ancient Chaos, reduced it to mere oceans, then wrapped those newborn seas in swaddling clothes of darkness mist and cloud?

who cut them off abrupt at the edge of land, whose law walls them off with a shore,

who ruled their proud swollen waters could only raise their foaming heads so high, no further?

Did *you* one day ordain that morning would exist and teach Dawn where to rise,

how her beams would seize the earth to its edges, scaring off crooks, making muggers hide from light?

clearing that crew from the newlit planet like you'd shake crumbs from a blanket,

making this world stand out sharp, distinct, like an image fresh-stamped in clay, in clear contour and high relief, shining and clothed with color,

denying the evil any pleasure in her light — which catches them in the arrogant act and breaks their upraised arm?

The Unholy Bible

Have you visited the springs that feed the sea from beneath, walked the weedy forests of the ocean floor?

Have you seen the gates of Sheol open? Even peered through its keyhole at Mot and the race of shades?

Do you understand how wide the world actually is? Tell me, if you've grasped it all!

What road leads to the home of Light, and Darkness — where's *its* house?

Trace these back to their native lands — lead on! you of course know the way,

you *must* know — you're so ancient, so great in days, born before either of these!

Have you been to the treasury where snow is stored, where I stockpile hailstones — at least you've seen *that*?

the icy armory where I save my skyish weapons for winter's bitter, war's chilling, day?

Why isn't light lessened, made fainter as it travels, scattering Eastern brilliance to the edges of the West?

Who pours the upper sky's flood down as rainfall, spraying it evenly over all between horizons? How do thunder and lightning know which way to roll and jag?

Who sends rain, now to the desert, where there's no man to even see it,

now quenching heat-cracked dusty fields to make them bristle fiercely green?

Does the rain have a father? Who gives birth to dew drops? Whose womb creates ice? Who's the mother of all frost?

How is it water freezes, disguising itself as translucent rock? The ocean itself cramps into white and solid plains!

Did you weave the Pleiades together, can you unfasten the stars of Orion's belt?

Do you make the zodiac roll forward with the seasons? can you console the Great Bear for never being able to

Job

touch her own cub?

Do you know the laws of the Heavens? Did you impose their influence on earth?

Can you raise your voice till it echoes through the clouds and they answer you in rainfall?

Do the lightning bolts wait for your orders, crackle out "Yes, Master!" and flash off where you send them?

Who placed wisdom behind the eyes, trapped insight in the skull's bone walls?

Whose intelligence marshals the armies of the clouds, at whose orders do they open fire — pouring out their weight in rain,

making dirt melt into autumn mud when summer suns have baked it hard as clay in a kiln?

Do you hunt up kills for the lion? fill their bellies with torn red flesh

when they've waited hungry hours crouched in their mountainside caves, in patient unfed ambush?

Who sees to it the raven finds food, when her children chirp to God that they're starving, and flutter in circles, giddy with hunger?

(39)

Did you decide the right season for mountain-goats to give birth? Do you midwive the pregnant deer when they crouch to squeeze out their babies, wombs widening pang by pang?

Their children grow and strengthen fast as the grass they feed on, they run off, forgetting they ever had a parent.

Who made the wild ass free from the first, never to know the bridle — to create him was to liberate him —

his home is every open field, every outstretch of desert's his address,

The Unholy Bible

he whinnies a jeer at the crowded towns; he'll never obey a mule-driver's shout,

he finds his pasture even on mountaintops, there's no plant he can't eagerly eat.

Does the buffalo wish he could be your slave? will he eat from a manger and sleep in a stall?

will you hitch him to your plough and have him pull furrows down your field?

will you trust him because he's so strong, count on his power to get your work done?

can you depend on him to bring in your harvest and thresh the sheaves of grain?

The ostrich, when she's happy, paddles her stubby wings — the stork's no less a bird with feathers to flash —

but only the ostrich lays and leaves her eggs lying out on the ground, trusting the dust to keep them warm,

she's no idea that every passing step, every beast of the field could crush them.

If she even recalled her children you could say she was cruel — but the laying of her eggs is less than a memory — if she noticed them now, she'd wonder what they were:

God shared no wisdom with her, but gave her a gap for a brain —

she flutters her useless wings and thinks she's flying, honks scornfully down at rider and horse.

Are you the one who made the horse strong? Did you weave the quivering muscles of his tremendous neck?

Did you teach him how to jump like a grasshopper? to snort scarily with his glorious big nostrils?

He scoops out a valley with impatient pawing hoof, whinnies his joy, gallops with all his power to meet the war-chariots;

if he knew what fear was, he'd laugh at it — he'll never swerve back from a sword.

Job

While arrows clank in the quiver on his saddle, spears hiss flickering by and javelins snap,

he drinks up distance, hurtling heavy over the quaking battered earth under hoof; when he hears the shofar-blast, he thinks it's another horse

and neighs back glad answer; he snuffs eagerly at the battle-smell, ears up for the shouting of war-horns and roaring of commands.

Did you instruct the hawk how to soar and circle with outspread wings?

Did you command the eagle fly at a prouder pitch, build a more eminent nest,

live on utmost cliff, fall asleep nodding over chasm, make its watchtowering house on the fang-point apex of crag?

— from there it scans the plain for food through telescope eyes;

wherever there's flesh to tear, the eagle's already diving after it, to bring her beaky babies back fat hunks of bloody meat.

(40)

And Jah said to Job:

Does my aggrieved colleague have any objection to raise? Does God's prosecutor have anything to add?

Job answered:

I'm humbled to nothing — what can I say? I clamp my hands over my gaping astounded mouth.

Bad enough I spoke even once; I'm not about to try it twice.

The Jah went on from the midst of his hurricane:

Stand up like a man, buckle on your armor, I'll ask, you answer *me*:

Are you really going to tell me my justice adds up to nothing, will you prove I'm to blame and you're right?

The Unholy Bible

are you about to shake your sky-churning fist and utter thunder?

Go on, veil yourself in exalted splendor, robe yourself in glory and pride,

scatter the bomb-bursts of your wrath, catch every arrogant man and knock him to his knees,

detect all the proud and make them crawl, beat down the wicked where they stand,

make the earth swallow them all, cover their faces with dirt,

go on, do it all, you powerful being! I just can't wait to see it!

Now look at Behemoth, like you, my creation — he chews grass like an ox,

what power's in the beef of his massy rump, woven with the sinews of his belly!

His penis is tough and supple as a cedar, his boiler-plate scrotum hugs a pair of cannon-balls,

his bones are pipes of bronze locked into cast-iron flesh,

he is God's masterpiece — only his creator would dare to battle him.

He could just as well chomp the grass on the hills where every other grazing beast is glad to be,

but he'd rather look up at the lotus, his tonnage sunk in reedy swamp,

in the shade of lotus-shrubs, hidden by willows all around.

If the river suddenly flooded, he wouldn't be startled or even shift position — not if the entire Jordan gushed straight into his face.

Do you think you can walk up under Behemoth's eyes and pierce his nose for a ring like a bull's?

Can you drag up Leviathan with a fishing rod, snag his lower jaw and yank him gaping out?

bore through his mouth with a fish-hook and string him like a bead by the face?

Job

Will he flatter you, croaking for mercy as he flops on the
dock?

Will he sign a contract with you to become your slave forever?

Will you give him to your daughters to play with like a
song-bird leashed by the leg?

Will you haggle over his price as you sell him by hunks to
the retailers?

Can you prick his hide with a spear, make his neckless
head bristle harpoons?

Go on — step closer — just touch him — I bet your
thoughts have turned from war —

(41)

you won't be planning your victory celebration — when
the sight of him sends you running for cover.

The cruellest mercenary wouldn't risk catching his eye —
who could stand up to and stare back at him?

I made everything under heaven — what do I owe to anyone — who even existed before me?

so why should I silently listen to your self-obsessed if powerful expressions, your graceful though irrelevant turns of phrase?

Has anyone ever gutted Leviathan, parted the curtains of
his flesh? Who ever dared draw near his horizon-wide lips?

Who's knocked on the gates of his face, seen them open on
the terror of his teeth?

His sealed, tight-fitted scales glitter magnificent as a river
of shields,

one so close to the other not a breath could leak between them,

they stick together like brothers, hold fast and never give up.

His sneeze is a white blast of heat, his eyes are two dawns
side by side,

live coals shoot from his mouth as embers leap from a fire

The Unholy Bible

— when he smiles the escaping flames lick his lips,
   smoke geysers out of his nostrils like steam from a boiling kettle,
   his breath would kindle coals, his mouth is a gaping cremation.
   His backbone is the summation of strength, he radiates anguish and fear;
   the layers of his flesh are pressed so dense that nothing could budge his bulk,
   his heart is hard as fossil, solid as a lower millstone;
   when he surfaces, heroes hug each other in terror, their boat shatters and they splash in panic.
   Sword, javelin, slingstone, mail — nothing stands up to him.
   He treats iron like straw, brass like rotten wood,
   no arrow makes him dive for cover, a sling-stone does no more than a handful of grass,
   to him a club is a nutshell, he thinks it's funny when you shake your spear.
   He can stretch out on glass-jagged rocks, comfortable as a flat-bottomed barge drawn up on a muddy bank.
   He makes the whole ocean boil around him like a pot of stew on the fire,
   his creaming wake so foams the sea it all goes white like a human's hair,
   there's nothing on earth even like him, not nearly another so fearless a creature,
   this being looks down on all proudest things, king over the kings of beasts.

(42)

   And Job replied to God:
   I know you can do everything — your intentions are immediate acts —

Job

"Who," you ask, " by his lack of understanding darkens the deliberation?"

I spoke as I did because I didn't understand — never guessed how astounding, how baffling you are —

You say: " Listen to my words: I'll ask the questions, then you reply and enlighten me!"

All I knew about you was nothing more than rumor — now that I've seen with my own eyes —

I melt into a puddle of penitence, wishing I could just seep unnoticed into the dirt.

Now Jah had finished talking to Job and, turning to Eliphaz, he said: "My anger roars up against you and your two friends because you didn't speak correctly concerning me as did my servant Job. Now take seven bulls and seven rams, and sacrifice them for an atonement while my servant Job prays for you as intercessor: and as a favor to him I won't punish you for your stupid, inaccurate ideas about me."

So Eliphaz, Bildad and Zophar did as God told them, and God spared them as a favor to Job.

And God reversed again the fortunes of Job while he was praying on behalf of his friends, and gave him back double all he'd had before. All Job's brothers and sisters and former friends came to Job's house, brought food and ate with him, nodded, sympathized, comforted him for all the evil God had sent down on him, and everyone gave him a coin and a golden ring.

And God blessed Job's end more than he had his beginning, and Job had 14,000 sheep, 6,000 camels, 1,000 yoke of oxen, and 1,000 she-asses; he had three daughters whom he named Crystal, Chantilly and Amber: they were the most beautiful girls in the entire country and they had big dowries too.

Job lived for another 140 years, saw his children's children's children, and finally died, an old man content with the length of his life.

Elihu, a Note to *Job*

The speeches of Elihu are generally regarded as an interpolation, due to his absence from the preface and conclusion, and because his affirmation that the meaning of suffering is to bring self-knowledge is at variance with the book's conclusion that no theoretic solution is possible.[6] To this we may add stylistic differences: where the other speeches are poetic, Elihu's are merely tortuous. I have accordingly omitted Elihu's speeches, to the vast improvement of the book's coherence and dramatic power. Elihu's speeches are however worth examining in some detail, as the features which confirm their intrusive nature also reveal the principal differences between Archaic and Rabbinic Judaism.

I will here examine the *premises* he develops according to their content, rather than synopsising the entire argument. For the argument is simple — Job *has* sinned, should repent; God is merciful, &c. What is interesting is the novel nature of the sin *definition*, one entirely foreign to Job, his friends, and his God.

Above all Elihu advances a new conception of man: that of man as the *reasoner*, which is the one now in current use, and indeed the scientific term, *homo sapiens*. Reason provides the basis of Elihu's critique: he calls it *ruah El*, "the spirit of God," but its characteristics make it clear that reason is the only adequate translation. (For these citations I will use the *King James*

Job

Version, adapted for clarity and correctness.) Elihu justifies his butting in by:

But there is a spirit in man, and the inspiration of the Almighty giveth understanding.

The majority are not always wise, nor do the aged always understand what's right. (*Job* 32: 8–9.)

It will be remembered that the friends made no such appeal to personal understanding, but only to customary belief, the experience of elders, etc. It should also be noted that Elihu's knowledge is drawn directly from the spirit of God in man: since he isn't claiming prophetic insight, reason seems the only explanation, one which is confirmed a little later when Elihu expands on this definition of *ruah.* He says:

My words shall be from the correctness of my thought, my lips shall speak pure knowledge:

the inspiration of God who made me, the spirit of God who makes me live. (*Job* 33: 3–4)

This "pure knowledge," *ðaat barur,* that is superior to customary belief is clearly to be read as Reason.

The definition of man as a rational being entails a distinction made between him and the animals "who want discourse of reason." Thus:

But none saith, where is God my maker, who giveth songs (i.e., instruction) in the night,

who teaches us more than the beasts of the earth, and maketh us wiser than the fowl of heaven. (*Job* 35: 10–11)

It will be remembered that there was no previous mention of man being qualitatively different from animals in this book, or in the *Genesis* account of man's creation. There man was given dominion over the beasts by God's simple fiat: only after rational psychology is accepted is this kind of distinction pointedly made. That man's rule over the animals was regarded as God's inexplicable will and not the result of Man's

The Unholy Bible

inherent rational superiority is clear from:

What is man that thou art mindful of him? and the son of man that thou visitest him?

For thou has made him a little lower than the angels, and hast crowned him with glory and honor.

Thou madest him to have dominion over the works of thy hands: thou has put all things under his feet. (*Ps.* 8:4–6)

We cannot fairly read the phrase "a little lower than the angels" as implying more than superior rank and dominion (which is in fact the explicit sense of line six). If man were viewed as being divinely imbued with Reason, we would scarcely find the self-deprecating question "What is man?" Rather we would encounter something on the order of:

What a piece of work is man, how noble in reason, how infinite in faculties, in form and moving, how express and admirable in action, how like an angel in apprehension, how like a god! the beauty of the world; the paragon of animals.... (*Hamlet*, 2:303–307)

Elihu's descriptions of God's nature are of a piece with his definition of Man as participant in God's intelligence ("the inspiration of the Almighty," *ruah el*, cited above from *Job* 32:8). When Elihu dismisses Job's complaints on the grounds that God *cannot* be unjust (Chapter 34), he does not appeal to traditional belief as the friends do, but says:

If God hated justice, how could he rule? (*Job* 34:17)

The idea is that God, insofar as he is all-powerful, must necessarily be just. The most puissant is by definition the best, the most good. Truly a definition in the manner of Plato, an abstract proof. But the logical formulation of God's nature is not our sole evidence that a God like Plato's is intended: he is explicitly defined as the supreme Intelligence:

Job

Behold, God is mighty, and despiseth not any, he is mighty through the power of his mind. (*Job* 36:5)

God is also defined as the source of intelligence in humans:

Behold, God is exalted in his power: who is a greater teacher (*moreh*) than he? (*Job* 36:22)

The highest power, the most good, the supremely wise and the source of wisdom: this concept is Greek, not Hebrew, in its formulation and content, and constitutes a complete break with earlier Hebrew tradition up to and including *Job*. By the time Elihu's speeches were written, Israel had been for perhaps a century under Greek rule, and Greek was the *lingua franca* — thus we cannot escape the conclusion we are dealing with direct Greek philosophic influence (though this is universally denied by Bible scholars).

What is most significant about this exaltation of reason is what is opposed to it. Job has said to God:

Why do you contend with a man but refuse to reply to his words? (*Job* 33:13)

to which Elihu counters:

In a dream, in a vision of the night, when deep sleep falls upon men, in slumberings upon the bed,

then he opens the ears of men which he sealed against warning and instruction;

in order that he might pervert their doings, God makes it impossible for a man to recognize his own arrogance. (*Job* 33:15–17)

Not actual crime but arrogance is now the focus of sin's definition. A variety of words are used for it: here *gewah*, elsewhere *gaon*, *pash* etc., but the sense is identical. This obsession with self-will is the necessary result of the redefinition of Man as "the Reasoner." Once rationality becomes the queen of the faculties, its opponent is the non-rational in Man: desire, passion, willfulness. This is like the Greek *hubris*, a par-

The Unholy Bible

ticularly apt parallel, since it was Greek rationalism that brought *hubris* into such prominence in Greek thought, and the same Greek rationalism. spread by Hellenism, that now brought the same dualistic rational psychology into Israel.

That a dream is the vehicle of God's instruction in no wise undermines the rational nature of the information it conveys. The concept of God perverting man's logic in order to punish him, then coaxing his reflection during sleep, is found in almost the same terms in — Aeschylus:

Zeus, who makes mortals understand, teaching by grief.
There is no other way.

Sleepwalkers! we try to go on living unaware
but pain keeps rapping at our skulls, shaking up memories,
till, imperceptibly, our eyes begin to open
and somehow, unwillingly, we start to see —
they do us this brutal favor, the holy all-controlling gods.

(Aeschylus, *Agamemnon*, 176–183)

The Hebrew view, and that of Job and his friends, was entirely different: there, God's commandments are revealed, and one may be punished for disobeying them but it is unimaginable that God would beat men into *inferring* them. In the Greek case, where traditional *mores* had never been explicitly codified, and rationalism had eroded the prestige (and even the memory) of custom, the law would have to be inferred — and just such systematic inference constitutes Plato's most extensive works.

To return to our exposition of the central place the "hubris" concept occupies in the Elihu speeches, we have Chapter 35, where Elihu gives a general description of the punishment of the wicked, and in which he shows that not only in Job's case but as a universal principle it is *hubris* that calls forth God's punishment.

There they (the wicked) cry, but none giveth answer,

122

Job

because of their sinful pride (*gaon,*)

surely God will not hear their vain (*shaw*) words, neither will the Almighty regard it.

Although thou sayest thou cannot discern his presence, he is judging, tremble and wait.

Do you think his anger punishes for nothing? that he doesn't know your great arrogance (*pash*)? (*Job* 35:12–15)

and later:

If a men be bound in fetters and be holden in cords of affliction,

then he showeth to them their work and their transgression brought about by their arrogance (*yithgabaru,*)

he openeth their ear to instruction and commandeth that they return from iniquity.

If they obey and serve him, they shall spend their days in prosperity and their years in pleasures.

But if they will not listen, they shall perish by the sword, and they shall perish according as they lack understanding. (*Job* 36:8–12)

And when Elihu actually describes Job's sin, he says:

Indeed, God led you astray, by taking you from poverty; you had much, without any lack, you sat at a rich table

and were full of condemnation of the wicked, you enjoyed how justly they were punished;

indeed, you suffer God's wrath because your God-given abundance seduced you, and now your wealth can't ransom you. (*Job* 36:16–18)

The difference between these and the friends' calls for repentance is that they assumed he'd actually *done* something. According to Elihu, the crime at issue is the interior one of arrogance.

Here we may observe the price of the defining Man as "The Reasoner." Because the definition of man as the Rea-

123

The Unholy Bible

soner is a partial one, because it leaves out imagination, passion, etc., it presents an inhuman and unattainable ideal. No man will achieve robotic self-mastery, accordingly every man falls short of "perfection." Man is saddled then with a false definition and criticized for failing to live up to it!

Elihu maintains God's absolute justice at the expense of a diminished definition of man: Man as Reasoner — but bad at it. In case of complaint one (here Elihu) merely counters:

Behold, God is great; we do not understand him. (*Job* 36:26)

That is, since man has not perfect rational wisdom, he cannot appreciate or criticize any of the ways of God. Whereas for the Hebrews Man was God's viceregent, for the Hellenized he became God's privileged ignoramus. This is the Greek view, and incidentally Paul's view — that humans are flawed, that they cannot attain righteousness. The Hebrew Kingdom view, and in any event Job's view, is that good action (which involves the entire person) is what counts, not the intricacies of motivation.

Nothing like the above reflections have ever been advanced, nor could they have been by the interested scholars: Christianity and Rabbinic Judaism accept Elihu's major premises as outlined above, and the standard scholarly reading follows suit, reading God's reply as setting "...before Job the madness of his insolence by pointing him to the mystery of natural occurrences which surpass all human insight and ability..."[7] This is nothing more than a fudged version of Elihu's interpretation: that Job is at fault due to ignorance and arrogance. It is therefore hardly a surprise that no attention has been give to how the *content* of Elihu's speeches substantiates more formal evidence of their insertion. Quite to the contrary, every effort has been directed at making Job's and God's speeches fit in with Elihu's model. It is for this reason that no

124

Job

adequate translation of the book exists.

At the root is an unwillingness to accept the profound influence of Greek thought on pre-rabbinic Judaism, *though an awareness of this is essential for understanding texts such as the Elihu speeches, Ecclesiastes and Deuteronomy.* So great is the prestige of the Abrahamic heritage that Jew and Christian alike have refused for two thousand years to acknowledge the mighty effect of Hellenism on Hebrew culture, even though that effect is recognized as a watershed in the history of all the (other) nations which experienced it, from Egypt to India.

5
Solomon's Testimony

This is in some ways the most difficult book to translate in the Hebrew Bible. Though the text is in generally an excellent state of preservation, the language is so elliptical that some lines are now quite unintelligible. This stylistic problem is exacerbated by the fact that we are now (3rd century BC) at the very border between Classical and Mishnaic Hebrew, and the different worlds they represent. The content of the Testimony is abstract and philosophical, but the vocabulary remains concrete and poetical — a rich store of abstract nouns such as we find in later Hebrew are not yet available. Often only the context tells us what abstract sense the concrete term is carrying. Our method has been to preserve the poetic language insofar as possible, but place glossingly beside it the abstract sense. For example, hevel "wind," may indicate anything from actual wind to concepts such as futility, uselessness, impassivity, endlessness or activity.

The famous opening line "vanity of vanities, all is vanity" actually reads "wind of wind, it's all wind." Since the following lines cite a devastating list of instances of activity, human and natural, being without lasting effect, we translate our "wind of wind" as "nothing lasts any longer than words shouted into the wind." Thus, by a periphrasis, we bring out the full content of the line without (we hope) forfeiting its poetic charm.

The Unholy Bible

A much subtler problem is the author's use of religious terms in a very non-religious way, for example he may use "righteous" to indicate "lucky." Here the sense is left deliberately and a little wickedly double: the author makes the limits of language a smoke-screen for his skeptical ideas. Unfortunately this delphic style cannot be matched in a translation that aims for clarity — much that I have had to translate as raw cynicism is expressed in the text by the verbal equivalent of a mysterious grin.

I have put into somewhat higher relief the book's clear implication that it was written by Solomon, sufficiently evident by the reference to predecessors on the throne, building projects, etc. This attribution was of course only to give the book prestige and authority — such apocryphal ascriptions were the rule rather than the exception for this period.

The customary title given the book, *Ecclesiastes*, is merely the Greek translation of the Hebrew title *Qoheleth*, and means "one who speaks before an assembly," a term with both religious and legal/political overtones. The English word *testimony* conveys precisely the sense required.

The actual author was evidently a wealthy man who had (by the tenor of his most-iterated complaints) been deprived of some of his income. He also shows a minute acquaintance with the down-side of court life, which suggests he was "passed over" for some deserved preferment. His overall tone is Epicurean, and it is entirely reasonable to assume that there was some direct influence: Epicurus himself lived from 342–271 BC, and Israel was under Greek rule from Alexander's conquest in 332 (taking it from Persia) to the age of Roman rule (with Pompey's conquest in 63 BC). Greek rule differed from Persian in that while the Persians were content to receive the taxes and leave it at that, the Greeks made a real attempt to incorporate the subject lands into the world of Hel-

128

Solomon's Testimony

lenic culture and politics — which meant that Greek was the language of all official business and became at least as well known in Israel as English is today. Accordingly, the author of this 3rd century BC Testimony was born into a hundred-year-old acquaintance with Greek culture, of which Epicureanism would have been one of the most powerful intellectual currents. Some of our author's statements on the indifference of God, the calm disposition advocated as a philosophical ideal, and the bland acceptance of death, are in content and formulation entirely Epicurean. This has of course been strenuously denied by the Jews, who have no interest in acknowledging the huge debt of late-classical and Rabbinic Hebrew thought to Greek culture, and by the Christians, who are even more eager to maintain the imagined "purity" of the Hebrew tradition, from which they claim a no less imaginary descent. Accordingly, this is the first translation ever to present honestly the Epicurean passages of this book.

We do not, however, wish to suggest that we have here to do with a simple Epicure. Though the author was unquestionably influenced by Epicurus' doctrine, his position probably represents that of the Sadducees, whose pointed hostility to the doctrine of life after death and the Pharisaic predilection for meticulous and wordy observance would have found much that was congenial in Epicurus' doctrines. When we remember that the Sadducees, the wealthy, priestly party, were also the Hellenizing "modernisers" from whom the Pharisees distanced themselves, the reading of the book as Epicurean-Sadducean becomes quite defensible.

The connection of the book with the Sadducees is a new one — the "official," pietised versions and interpretations of the text passed along from generation to generation have prevented this clear identification.[8]

The Unholy Bible

The Testimony of Solomon, Son of David, King in Jerusalem

(Chapter 1) It's all pointless, declared the king, nothing lasts any longer than words shouted into the wind.

What do men get for all their hard labor in the few days they're given to live under the sun? What's left to show for it all?

The generations come and go, leaving not so much as a footprint behind them on the earth

which lasts impassively forever.

The sun rises, the sun goes down, then rushes underground back to the place it started and rises blithely there again as though it never had before;

the wind blows south, then veers back north, circling, circling, around and back again forever;

all rivers flow always to the sea, which never gets any fuller, but they keep on pouring oceanwards, just like they always have;

it's demoralizing even to contemplate all this unrelenting but meaningless activity — it's exhausting even to try and describe it —

and even if one could, it would do no good — the eye will never be sated with seeing, however much the ears have heard they're still hungry to hear more:

we're forever eager to find out something further, something new, even though there's nothing that will be or be done that isn't the same thing all over again — there's nothing really new under the sun.

Solomon's Testimony

Whenever someone says: "Look, *this* at least is new!"

you can be sure it's only something so old that everyone's forgot the last time it happened.

No one remembers the first human beings, nor will there be any better recollection of this present generation among those who live in the times that are to come.

I, Solomon, who testify, was the last to rule from Jerusalem over a united Israel;

I set my mind to explore and dispassionately examine every activity that takes place under the heavens:

all in all, it's a sorry business that God gave man to slave over.

I reviewed every possible mortal employment the sun so briefly shines upon — and discovered that not one has more, or better, or longer effect than writing on sand or shouting words into the wind.

There's more wrong in this world than human work can fix, too much even to set down in a list.

So I said to myself: "I've accumulated more power and wisdom than any king who ruled before me in Jerusalem, my mind has far explored along the paths of Wisdom and Experience;

let me now, for the sake of comparison, try insane self-indulgence and hunt unthinkingly for pleasures, to see if that's equally useless and deluded,

since I've found that Wisdom just makes you more irritable, and understanding why things happen just makes you sadder.

(Chapter 2) So I resolved to pop the joyful cork and start the party

— this proved equally empty —

wine made me howl with laughter over nothing, ecstatically happy for no reason at all

— this did not however change anything.

The Unholy Bible

So I tried a more moderate indulgence in wine, and continued my grim driven grasping after whatever secrets the pleasures might contain — perhaps they'd reveal the best way for man to spend his few years of life here on earth.

I undertook massive building projects, erected palaces, planted vineyards,
made gardens and parks, planting them with every species of fruit tree,
I had dug fishponds — actually, lakes, — big enough to water my new-planted forests now transplanted to their shores, where none had ever been before,
I had slaves and slave-girls, some bought, some born to those already on my estates; I had more cattle and sheep than all my predecessors at Jerusalem together;
I stockpiled gold and silver: my private holdings exceeded those of provinces, of kingdoms;
I had male and female singers, and, that greatest of pleasures known to Adam's sons — wives and mistresses.
I became greater and richer than any king before me in Jerusalem — my wisdom was useful for this at least.
I never denied myself any enjoyment — and indeed, these bursts of pleasure in the midst of all my acquiring were the only pay-off for what was actually hard work.
Then I stood back and overviewed all my efforts and what they'd constructed;
I might just as well have slaved to build castles in the air for all the lasting worth my work had — nothing that's built in days can last more than a petty measure of suns.

Then I looked back on my exploration of wisdom and my soundings in senseless pleasure, with an eye to deciding which, on balance, was better,

Solomon's Testimony

trying to see things from the perspective of my successors in the far future calmly reviewing what was done by those before them —

and I saw there is more advantage in prudence and wisdom than there is in the insane hunt for fun, just as there's more advantage in having a light than there is in stumbling around in the dark;

the wise man at least has his eyes in his head, the fool might as well be blind.

But I also noted that neither escapes death, a like end comes to them both, and I thought:

"I'm going to die, the same as any moron, so what good is there in having been so wise? It didn't provide a way out of death, which will dissipate my accumulated wisdom like smoke into the wind.

"the wise aren't remembered forever, in fact little longer than fools.

"In the unending outstretch of days to come everything is finally forgotten — the wise and the fool, equally dead, are just as unremembered as if neither had lived."

So I hated life, because it looked to me a bad business, the whole deal, this moment, this flicker of existence in sunlight

since all our efforts are finally meaningless as breeze, which, whether it pass by whispering or roaring, leaves no lasting track and signifies nothing.

And I was even more disgusted with all I'd built up in my short term here on earth, under the sun, since I'd only end up leaving it to the man who comes after me —

a man who could be stupid or brilliant — I'll never know — and he'll have control over all my laborious works which I planned so intelligently all my life's short day — efforts as meaningless finally as the wind stirring the sand.

The Unholy Bible

Thus disgusted, I turned away, and gave up even thinking about all the great works I'd done in my mortal sum of suns,
   since a man who's worked carefully, intelligently and successfully has to give it all to someone who made no effort for it:
   that's not only meaningless as breeze, it's terribly wrong.

What then does a man get for all his work and anxious plannings all his brief number of suns?
   He gets to have all his days made sad and irritable from overwork, and worries that keep him awake at night
   — a life that comes and goes insignificant as wind.

Does a righteous life then consist in eating and drinking and trying to enjoy yourself despite your life's workload?
   Those *do* seem to be the terms on which God handed us this existence:
   and certainly, pleasure comes from God, regardless of whether Man decides to enjoy or refrain.
   I don't see how we can avoid the conclusion that the good man, the man with whom God is pleased, is the one whom God gave enough wisdom and experience to enjoy himself,
   and the sinner, if this is at all a meaningful term, must be the one God punishes by leading him to labor to amass and gather all sorts of possessions which he ends up leaving to another —
   to another, whose effortless acquisition of the stuff shows *he's* the one who's righteous and rightly rewarded.
   Well, if that's the way things are, then working hard to heap up holdings is as useful as trying to herd the clouds.
   (Chapter 3) In this world of things so short-lived and fast shifting that time is reckoned by suns, there's no intention or activity that doesn't soon find its necessity and appropriate moment.

Solomon's Testimony

Suddenly it's the right time to give birth or to die, to plant or tear out by the roots, to murder or heal, kick down or build up, cry or laugh, grieve or dance, save or squander, make love or refrain, seek out or get rid of, guard or neglect, tear up or sew together, keep quiet or speak, love or hate, make war or peace —

Since life is such a frantic succession of changes, such a storm of altering circumstances, how can any work a man undertakes help him for long?

And I pondered the various sorts of work God gave Adam's heirs to slave over:

God made every kind of activity as a beautiful match to a certain need and circumstance,

and he gave man an intelligence great enough to contemplate the whole world,

without however giving him the kind of insight that would enable him to uncover the underlying causes and ultimate ends of the events God causes to occur. Consequently, man never knows for sure what will happen next,

and the best he can expect from any work is to have some pleasure in doing it and to earn a living by it.

Indeed, any pleasure from food or drink or general contentment a man can extort from his life-sentence of hard labor — that's a gift from God, in fact the only one he gives.

And I understood that God will forever continue to run the world exactly as he does now; no change can possibly be effected in the pattern of existence for better or for worse: we can do no more than look on in amazement;

that which was once is no different from the yet more distant past, and what will be will repeat what once was —

God is apparently chasing himself in circles.

The Unholy Bible

I also noted these features of mortal existence:

in place of fair decision there was injustice, and in place of equity, evil.

At first I thought: "Eventually God will have to judge between the righteous and the guilty; like everything else in turn, justice will find its necessity and appropriate moment."

But I was finally forced to conclude that if any divine decision is to be deduced from the lack of justice in the world,

it's only the decision to demonstrate that men's contendings in no way differ from the amoral survival-fights of animals.

And in fact, the same end comes to man and beast, they die alike:

man is no better than beast, the same breath pumps through human and animal lungs, and when they breathe their last both their souls dissipate into the wind, and both their bodies go under the same earth.

All living things are made out of dirt, to dirt they return. No one really *knows* that the human soul rises skywards while that of an animal just seeps into the ground.

I conclude then that there is nothing better for a human than to try and take pleasure in what he does — because that much surely *is* given him,

and there's no way of knowing what — if anything — happens after death.

(Chapter 4) When I turned my attention to all the oppression that takes place here on earth throughout life's brief sun-measured stretch of days:

I saw the tears of the victim, and how everyone just ignored them,

and as for the oppressors, they had power, but no one had any warm feelings for them either.

And I envied those who'd died long ago, at least more than I did those still living

Solomon's Testimony

— but luckier than either are those who haven't yet been born, who've never had to see what a rotten business it is, this mortal existence under a short succession of suns.

Pondering all the hard work that men do and the profits they make from their labor, I saw that it was all motivated by competitive envy — which is meaningless as breeze and about as sensible as trying to herd clouds.

But on the other hand, the lazy fool just lies on his back and snores his way to starvation.

All in all, it's better to own little and enjoy it, to have one scant handful of contentment, than to sweat and stagger under a double armload of work and possessions and never have pleasure from them.

Another human condition I saw which made no sense at all was a man all alone, without even a brother, ceaselessly slaving away, never rich in his own eyes no matter how wealthy he was, never asking himself for whom he was spurning delights and living laborious days —

that's crazy, and it's sad.

Two together are better off than one alone: their shared expenses are easier to meet,

and if one falls, the other can help him up — but if you fall alone, who'll hold out a hand to you?

Two sleeping together keep each other warm; it's a shivery business sleeping alone.

If some one attacks you, you and your friend could stand up to him easy, and three cords braided together make a rope that won't soon snap.

A boy who's poor but smart is better than a king who's old and foolish and has forgotten how to listen to advice —

The Unholy Bible

because that poor boy may yet make it as far as from the jail to the throne of the country he was born in, while the old foolish king may yet lose all he was born to.

[*lines 4:15–16 unintelligible.*]

(Chapter 5) Don't be in a hurry to utter vows before God or even think them. God is the Lord of Heaven, and you're a little creature scurrying on earth. Have a sense of your scale in the scheme of things and let your words be few.

Just as a dream rushes forward filled with unrelated matters, the voice of a fool in prayer is full of empty promises and silly wishes.

When you *do* vow an offering to God, don't put off its fulfillment. God doesn't like to be toyed with by fools: if you vow it, do it and soon! It's better to have made no vow at all than to fail to fulfill it once made.

Don't let your unthinking tongue bring punishment down on your whole body, don't have to explain to the recording angel it's all a mistake.

Why should God come to hate the sound of your voice and ruin your business as punishment because your jabber was empty and senseless as the words of a man talking in his sleep?

Show God some respect.

Don't be stunned when you see the poor crushed, justice stolen and judicial decision for sale in the land: society is a pyramid of oppression, every high-placed predator has another over him. Whatever the land produces has to be split up among them all — and so it comes about that there's not a weed in a vacant lot the government doesn't tax.

The man who loves money will never have enough to be contented, nor can the man who loves property ever be satis-

Solomon's Testimony

fied by more. Acquisition by itself is finally senseless.

The more you have, the more hired people you have eating it up, until you as owner have to spend all your time managing things, and have no advantage over your employees,

except the empty one of being able to look it all over and think "mine."

Sleep is sweet for a working man no matter how small his supper was, while the rich man with his full belly lies awake worrying.

There is a sickeningly evil thing I've seen here on earth: you have a man who denied himself, suffered privations to save up a lot of money, then he loses the whole hoard in a bad business deal,

and he ends up leaving his child empty-handed, and he himself dies naked and poor as a newborn babe, not a penny left in his fist for all the work he did.

This is disgustingly unjust! He leaves life the same as he entered it, with nothing to show for all his pointless labor,

the dinners he ate in the dark to save a candle, his suffering, frustration and rage.

So then, this is what I found to be good and appropriate for a human to do in life — to eat and drink and try to enjoy whatever work he does here on earth for the short sum of suns God's allotted him.

The man to whom God gives wealth and property, and the power to use and enjoy what he has and take pleasure in his work — that's the man whom God has blessed.

God gives Man happiness to counterbalance the fact that his life is short and he knows it.

The Unholy Bible

(Chapter 6) There's an evil I've see here on earth — and a common one it is — you have a man whom God has given wealth, property and honor — there's nothing he could wish for that he doesn't have — and yet God doesn't let him enjoy what he's got — some stranger comes and takes it all.

It's insane that this can happen — and it's sickeningly unfair.

If a man have a hundred sons, and live a hundred years, but he doesn't get his portion of mortal enjoyment, if he ends up so poor and alone there's no one to even bury his bones — I'd say an abortion made out better than he did,

for it approached existence gently as a breath and returned whence it came quiet as night, it never left the shadows of nameless non-being; it never saw the sun or the kind of life that sunlight shows us

— that aborted almost is happier than a man who lives twice a thousand joyless years:

after death comes nothing for either, there's no afterworld compensation of a bitter life here.

(Chapter 7) There's no perfume smells better than a good reputation.

The day of death is better than the day someone's born, and it's better to go to a funeral than to a party — because it makes you remember that you, like everyone else, are going to die.

Tears are better than laughter, and sad looks are a sign you're starting to understand things.

The wise man's mind is always half-grieving, the fool's is amused at everything.

It's better to listen to a wise man scold you than to tap your feet to the songs of fools — the laughter of the fool is a meaningless noise, like the crackling of thorns thrown on hot coals.

Solomon's Testimony

[*7:7 unintelligible.*]

What's important is not how a thing starts, but how it ends.

A patient mind is better than one that's proud and quick to take offense: being always in a huff is the mark of a fool.

Don't say "Things were better in the old days.." — That's a failure of pessimism — things never *were* good.

[*7:11–12 unintelligible.*]

Consider this world which God has made: who can set right all that God made wrong in it?
But this at least you *can* do: when things go well, enjoy. When things go badly, remember
God makes both success and misfortune, forever alternating, no man has any idea what's coming next — things may improve in turn.

In the course of my pointless life I've seen everything: just men most unjustly killed, evil men living evilly ever after.
Don't be too righteous or too wise — why get yourself destroyed?
Don't be too evil or unduly stupid — why should you die before your time?
Hold on to both these rules, careful not to grip just one and let the other drop,
but always be God-fearing, by which I mean, be circumspect — and everything should be fine.

A wise man is more powerful through his own prudence than the 10 most important men in the city —

The Unholy Bible

but remember, there's not a man in the world who's perfectly righteous, that is, who always makes the right choice with never an error.

Don't listen to everything people say — you might overhear your servant cursing you — and that's not worthy of our attention. You know that plenty of times you've said tart things about others you felt more than you meant.

Careful reflection also showed me the following to be true:
I resolved to become wise — but that proved beyond me.
Existence is too wide for a man to take it all in, so deep you'll never get to the bottom of it;
but in my attempts to explore the whole human condition, from wisdom and prudence, through wickedness and rashness down to madness and stupidity, I did however make this discovery:
that Death itself causes less suffering than Woman.
She's a trap — she uses love as a bait, and when she locks her arms around you, you can almost hear the cage-door clanging shut.
The man God has blessed is the one who escapes her, the man God wants to punish is the one she snares and enslaves.
This is my sworn testimony: I reckoned up all my experiences and this is the sum result:
I found maybe one decent man in a thousand, but not a single good woman yet, even though I've never stopped looking, and wish with my whole soul to find one.
But bear in mind this slightly counterbalancing consideration: so far as I can make out, God made all human beings basically upright, but they thereafter have, of themselves, proved unfortunately ingenious.

Solomon's Testimony

(Chapter 8)   What is the mark of a wise man, of one who understands why things occur?

Intelligence makes you smile, it lights up the face, gentles the expression and makes the eyes shine.

My advice to the courtier: obey the king, stay true to the oath you swore before God at the coronation.

When you attend him in court: don't panic and run out when he loses his temper, nor should you stand up to him when he's wrong;

he'll do whatever he wants anyway, its not like you can escape or change him.

The king's command is insuperable — who can say to him "What do you think *you're* doing?"

Obey orders and you'll stay out of trouble; play his game by his rules, use tact, remember etiquette, and you'll do very wisely.

Tact and timing will save almost any situation, but remember, the human condition has this great defect:

not only is it impossible to know what will happen next, even if you have a fair idea, there's no telling how soon.

No man can command the wind to stop, no man beats death, no man can take a break in the middle of a battle, and no evil man's evil will save him in the end.

I also made this observation in my study of all that takes place under the sun: it often falls out that one man has power over another and abuses it cruelly.

I've seen just such evil persons solemnly interred in holy ground and the funeral procession return sadly to the city — clearly the mourners were quite ready to forget all these men had done. Which is insane.

The Unholy Bible

If there's no prompt or even eventual redress for the evil men do,

then of course people feel encouraged to do wrong. They sin, they commit a hundred crimes — they know everyone will put up with it.

[*8:12b–13 a pious interpolation.*]

A further earthly condition that makes no sense:

there are honest men who suffer what criminals deserve, and crooks who get the rewards honesty earned.

Seeing how much on earth makes how little sense, I place the highest valuation on Pleasure;

there's nothing better for a mortal than to eat, drink and be glad. He should always have some joy to offset the drudgery God gave him for a life under so small a sum of suns.

Having set my mind to the acquisition of Wisdom and the examination of all earthly activities,

I concluded that even if a man were to keep poring over it all, sleepless, day and night, life-long,

he could still never come to understand all the things God causes to occur beneath the sky.

No matter how hard you search, the meaning of life will elude you, and if some wise man says he's found it, then you can be *quite* sure he hasn't.

(Chapter 9)   Reflecting intently on the pleased or angry reception God gives to the actions of even the wise and the just, I can only conclude God does whatever whim dictates — man can't predict how he'll react and any response is possible.

And in the end, Death gets everyone, the just man and the evil man, the good man who observes the laws of ritual purity

Solomon's Testimony

and the man who cares nothing about defilement, the one who sacrifices to God and the one who doesn't, Death comes to the virtuous just as to the sinner, the one who uses God's name just for emphasis same as the one who respects it —

of all the injustices under the sun, this one is the worst — that one same end comes equally to everyone:

this consideration fills mens minds with evil and madness while they live: why shouldn't they do as they please right now? they're all condemned to death no matter what.

But still, there's always hope for a man, as long as he's alive — bad as things may be, remember: a live dog is still better off than a dead lion.

True, the living know they will die — but the dead don't know *anything*.

The dead can't accept your gifts or hear your praise, their loves, their hates, and their jealousies were over long ago.

They have nevermore any effect on the doings of the world.

Get along then, sit yourself gladly to table, eat up, drink your cheerful wine,

for these pleasures are signs of God's favor as sure as anyone gets.

Dress up every day in silk, don't spare the rare perfume, enjoy life with the woman you love all the days of your meaningless existence,

for this is your portion, your wage for the long day's labor of life.

Everything you undertake — do it with all your might. This is your only chance to do it at all —

there's no doing or reasoning or learning or knowing in Sheol where you're going.

The Unholy Bible

The fastest man doesn't always win the race or the strongest man the battle,

often enough the revered scholar starves and even the shrewd man can't make a living,

when times get hard enough, not even a con-man can strike up a friendship. Chance and luck rule all.

Poor baffled Mankind can never tell the right moment when it comes,

so circumstances catch us like fish in the cruel net,

like birds in the trap — suddenly snared wherever bad luck jumps us.

Sunlight showed me this discovery too, and I think it no small one:

There was once a small, sparse-inhabited city, and a great king came and surrounded it, building huge siege-towers.

There lived in that city a man poor but wise, who had a plan that would have saved them. But no one would listen to him because he didn't look important.

And I realized: Wisdom may be stronger than an army, but when it wears a patched coat no one comes to listen,

even though its words are easier on the ear than the shouted commands of the idiot-in-chief.

Insight is better than weapons, but one fool's enough to wreck a well-laid plan, (Chapter 10) just as one dead fly in the perfume is enough to make the whole bottle ferment and stink,

and a single mistake can destroy a long earned reputation and people's belief in your wisdom.

Solomon's Testimony

A wise man's mind is his savior — that a fool thinks at all destroys him;
even when he's just walking down the street, the fool's every movement declares what he is.

If the ruler loses his temper with you, stand your ground, don't leave the room —
when he's done shouting, answer gentle and calm — this approach can win forgiveness for even big sins.

Another earthly evil I've noticed — which must be just an oversight on the part of our esteemed rulers —
for they wouldn't have knowingly given fools high office while men of name and property were humiliatingly ignored —
and yet, I have seen slaves on horseback while princes followed on foot...

If you dig a pit for a booby-trap, you may be the one who falls into it.
If you move the stones that mark the property lines, you may get bit by the snake that lives under them.

Dangerous work is called dangerous for a reason — every stone-quarrier and woodcutter can show you scars.

If you don't sharpen a dulled axe, you'll have to work harder: it makes more sense to use your brain — and your whetstone.

There's no point in knowing the art of snake-charming if the serpent bites you before you can use it.

A wise man's words win friends, a fool's mouth is so dangerous to himself it would be an act of charity to gag him:

The Unholy Bible

he starts by uttering nonsense, talks his way into bad trouble — and he still has lots more to say.

A man never fully grasps what's happening right now — so he needs someone to read him the future?

Fools work hard at working too hard — it takes effort to always avoid the clear, well-beaten path.

I'm sorry for the country whose king is a boy and whose court begins feasting in the morning,
and I envy the country whose king acts like a nobleman should, whose courtiers come to table at the appropriate time, to satisfy their well-earned hunger, not to get drunk.

It's neglect, not bad wood, that makes the roof sag and leak.

Food, it's true, was made for feasting, and wine to make life glad — yes,
and money was made for a man to earn, without it you won't drink *or* eat.

Don't curse the king even in your thoughts, don't bad-mouth the powerful in your own bed under the covers —
the stool-pigeon builds its nest where you'd lest expect it, and can make your private thoughts well-known as a popular song.

(Chapter 11) It's worth the risk of shipping your merchandise overseas for the profit it'll eventually get,
but entrust your goods to seven or eight different vessels — here on earth one never knows what disaster is about to occur.

Solomon's Testimony

When the clouds gather and blacken, they're about to empty their rain onto earth;

no matter which direction a tree falls, where it falls is where it lies:

there is an ineluctable logic to the way things happen — don't expect Reality to change its rules for you.

If you're forever watching the weather for the most favorable time, you'll never get around to planting — much less reaping.

You can't see what the wind is bringing any more than you can see what kind of baby's taking shape in a woman's pregnant belly,

nor can you second-guess what God has in store for the world.

Sow your seed in the morning, and don't stop work till it's too dark to see:

you can't tell which seed will sprout, which won't — maybe all of them will grow up strong.

Light is immediately sweet and directly a pleasure — how good it is to look at the sunlit world —

always try to be happy, for as many years as you live —

it may help if you keep in mind how many years you won't live — the endless nothingness to come.

To be young is a victory. Hooray for the head without white hairs!

Whatever you wish for or like the look of — try and win it right now —

remember, by the laws of this world all delights are condemned to die — and soon.

Avoid anger and sorrow just as seriously as you'd take precautions not to get sick.

The Unholy Bible

What could be worth the time lost to tears now, in your youth, which goes by fast as wind and leaves as little trace?

(Chapter 12)   Remember your creator, now, in your youth, before old painful age comes and you can't enjoy a thing anymore,
before the sun, moon and stars look dull to your eyes grown dark from a lifetime's tears,
and the heavy clouds never leave your sky,
before those sentries of your house, your arms, tremble with age, and those brawny servants, your legs, are stooped under the weight of years,
and your teeth, the women who grind your grain, are too few to do the work, and lights are going out in the window of your eyes,
and your ears, those doors open on the marketplace, are shut, muffling it all to a distant din,
and while you can't hear the birds any more, your own voice becomes a shrill chirp,
and you look up with dread at a hill ahead, and a short walk has its dangers,
and your head whitens like an almond tree in blossom, and your cock won't stand up to crow, and the nuts that hang from your branch are stale and good for nothing,
and you're about to change your address for the final time, and the undertaker walks past your house every day;
while the golden lamp of life still burns, hanging from its silver chain — before that chain snaps and the lamp is smashed —
while the bucket still draws you up waters of life from the well of existence,
before your clay melts back into the earth it was shaped from,

Solomon's Testimony

and your breath returns to God who lent it,

— remember your creator, now, in your youth, and what he has in store for you, and realise that everything is breeze-meaningless, fast-passing, traceless, air-empty.

This is my sworn testimony.

I who write these lines was not only a sage but a teacher;

I collected wise sayings, tested them all, and set down the best —

those which went to the heart of the matter, which told the honest truth.

The sayings of the wise are like spurs...

[*12:11b–c unintelligible*]

One final piece of advice, my child:

writing books is an endless task — you'll never say it all,

and studying books will exhaust you long before you know enough.

[*12:13–14 a pious interpolation.*]

Textual Notes

1 The standard title, *Psalms,* is from the Septuagint's Greek *Psalmoi,* literally "harp-string twangs," i.e., songs. I have preferred a more literal rendering.

2 This psalm shows influence from the polytheistic Canaanite culture the Hebrews encountered (and absorbed) in the Promised Land, especially clear from the use of the Canaanite names El (the Creator/Father of the gods) and Shamash (the Sun-god.) I omit lines 8 and on as these constitute a pious attempt to incorporate this poem in a meditation on the splendors of the Creation. Such contemplation of the material world as a manifestation of the one transcendent deity will not become a general style of piety until the Second Temple — a testimony to these last lines' later addition.

3 This poem speaks of Jah in the terms one would expect of the pastoral-nomadic ancestors of the Israelites. As the excellent condition of the text contradicts an assumption of unspeakable eld, we must assume this is a nostalgic allusion to the purer past by a poet living in civilised Canaan during the time of the Judges. I have been particularly literal in my rendering of the word for Death, "Mot," because it is the Canaanite name for the Death-god and as such would have been recognised by the contemporary reader — just as we would appreciate the mythological resonance of "Hades."

4 This may come as a minor surprise to the reader who is accustomed to thinking of the Hebrew concept of God as quite simply God. Nonetheless the Sky-God, who is the creator, makes a brief visit to the earth to give humanity its laws, is famous for his goodness

Textual Notes

and mercy, along with the features we shall here consider in detail, is, with exactly these characteristics, a universally attested religious Pattern, from Haitian Damballah through Canaanite El to the Chinese T'ien.

5 Chapters 32–37 are omitted as spurious. A synopsis of their content and proofs of their later insertion are offered at the end of *Job*.

6 Eissfeldt, *Old Testament*, p. 457.

7 Eissfeldt, *Old Testament*, p. 467.

8 There is some imprecision in our use of the terms Sadducee and Pharisee, which come to us from Josephus and the Greek Testament, that is, three or four hundred years after *Ecclesiastes* was written. The poverty of our sources for the history of post-exilic and pre-Roman Israel permits, indeed necessitates, our projection of the terms backwards in time. The proof that the proceeding is just is that the available materials, that is the *Mishna* for the Pharisees and *Ecclesiastes* for the Sadducees, show a precise identity with the later descriptions.

BIBLIOGRAPHICAL NOTES

The most radical thing about this translation is the acknowledgement of Greek influence on 3rd century BC Biblical literature. We have already stated our case in the "Elihu" essay following *Job* and in the preface to *Solomon's Testimony*: the demonstration lies in coherence of the translations.

Bible scholarship, Jewish and Christian alike, has unquestioningly accepted the Hannukah-story of the Hebrew religious tradition remaining "pure" of Hellenic influence. Useful surveys of this scholarship, showing the kinds of questions that *are* asked (primarily dating) are to be found in the relevant articles in *The Jewish Encyclopaedia* and Otto Eissfeldt's *The Old Testament, an Introduction* (trans. Ackroyd, Harper & Row, 1965).

As to the individual books we shall only cite those commentaries on which we have particularly relied. These were:

153

The Unholy Bible

King Solomon's Book of Love Songs:
The brilliant study by Robert Gordis, *The Song of Songs*, Texts and Studies of the Jewish Theological Seminary, NY 1955.

Psalms:
Having chosen the clearest compositions in the book, no secondary source or emendation was necessary.

How:
Nothing would have been possible without the superlative work of D. R. Hillers, *Lamentations*, Anchor Bible, Garden City, NY 1972. Where I differ from Hillers it is generally in rejecting emendations to prefer a more conservative reading.

Job:
Here I was entirely on my own, since all studies to date have focused on showing the author couldn't have possibly meant anything as shocking as what he clearly says. The text is late (4th–3rd century BCE), clear and requires no emendation.

Solomon's Testimony:
Here we relied somewhat on Robert Gordis' *Qoheleth, The Man and his World*, Shocken, NY, 1968, which is however primarily valuable for its preface with able arguments for a 3rd-century dating. Here as with *Job* however, much that Gordis (and perhaps he alone) could have solved remained elusive due to refusal on the part of all Bible scholars to accept the "impiety" of the text.

The principal difficulty the book presents is the decipherment of the delphic style. Most useful were standard compilations of traditional commentaries, such as Reichert and Cohen's *Ecclesiastes* in the Soncino *Five Megilloth*, London & Bournemouth, 1952, which gives one the benefit of a thousand years' attempts at interpreting the dark gnomic utterances in the book.

My text has been Kittel's *Biblia Hebraica Stutgartensia*, with the following emendations:

Bibliographical Notes

VARIANTS AND EMENDATIONS

Song of Solomon
1:7	בְּטֹעְיָה
2:4	דָּגְלוֹ
5:13	מִגְדָּלוֹת
6:4	בַּמִּגְדָּלוֹת

Lamentations
1:4	נוֹגוֹת
1:8	נִדָּה
1:11	מַחֲמַדֵּיהֶם
1:12	לְכוּ לָכֶם
1:13	יוֹרִידֶנָּה
1:14	נִשְׁקַד עַל
	עָלָה עֲלוּ עַל
1:15	סָלָל
1:20	שְׁמַע
2:13	אֶעֱרוֹךְ
2:14	שְׁבוּתֵךְ
2:18	צָעֲקִי
	נֶחֱמָת
2:19	delete last line (repet. of 2:11)
2:22	מְגוֹרְדַי
3:5	רֹאשׁ
3:14	עַמִּים
3:17	רִיזְנַח
3:20	וְתָשִׁיחַ
3:22	תַּמּוּ
3:26	כִּי יוֹחִיל
	omit ו of וְדוּמָם

The Unholy Bible

3:33	יַיֶּגֶה
3:41	עַל
3:51	עֵנִי ... מְכַלֶּה בְּנוֹת עֵנִי
3:56	לְשַׁוְעָתִי
4:1	יִשְׁנֶא
4:3	כַּיְעֵנִים
4:9	יָזוּבוּ
4:14	נְגֹאֲלוּ
4:16	חִלְּקָם
4:17	עֵרֵנוּ
5:5	עָלָה עַל
5:9	מְדַבֵּר "the sword speaks," i.e., martial law

▲ SEMIOTEXT(E) DOUBLE AGENTS SERIES ▲
JIM FLEMING & SYLVÈRE LOTRINGER, EDITORS

FATAL STRATEGIES
Jean Baudrillard

FOUCAULT LIVE
COLLECTED INTERVIEWS
Michel Foucault

ARCHEOLOGY OF VIOLENCE
Pierre Clastres

LOST DIMENSION
Paul Virilio

AESTHETICS OF DISAPPEARANCE
Paul Virilio

COLLECTED INTERVIEWS OF
WILLIAM S. BURROUGHS
William S. Burroughs

▲ SEMIOTEXT(E), THE JOURNAL ▲
JIM FLEMING & SYLVÈRE LOTRINGER, EDITORS

SEMIOTEXT(E) USA
Jim Fleming & Peter L. Wilson, eds.

OASIS
Timothy Maliqalim Simone, et al., eds.

SEMIOTEXT(E) CANADAS
Jordan Zinovich, ed.

POLYSEXUALITY
François Peraldi, ed.

SEMIOTEXT(E) ARCHITECTURE
Hraztan Zeitlian, ed.

SEMIOTEXT(E) SF
Rudy Rucker, Robert Anton Wilson,
Peter Lamborn Wilson, eds.

RADIOTEXT(E)
Neil Strauss & Dave Mandl, eds.

▲ SEMIOTEXT(E) FOREIGN AGENTS SERIES ▲
JIM FLEMING & SYLVÈRE LOTRINGER, EDITORS

POPULAR DEFENSE &
ECOLOGICAL STRUGGLES
Paul Virilio

SIMULATIONS
Jean Baudrillard

GERMANIA
Heiner Müller

COMMUNISTS LIKE US
Félix Guattari & Toni Negri

ECSTASY OF COMMUNICATION
Jean Baudrillard

STILL BLACK, STILL STRONG
Dhoruba Bin Wahad, Mumia
Abu-Jamal & Assata Shakur

FORGET FOUCAULT
Jean Baudrillard

ASSASSINATION RHAPSODY
Derek Pell

REMARKS ON MARX
Michel Foucault

DRIFTWORKS
Jean-François Lyotard

SPEED AND POLITICS
Paul Virilio

SADNESS AT LEAVING
Erje Ayden

PURE WAR
Paul Virilio & Sylvère Lotringer

LOOKING BACK
ON THE END OF THE WORLD
Jean Baudrillard, Paul Virilio, et al.

NOMADOLOGY
THE WAR MACHINE
Gilles Deleuze & Félix Guattari

METATRON
Sol Yurick

BOLO'BOLO
P.M.

ON THE LINE
Gilles Deleuze & Félix Guattari

WHAT IS CRITIQUE?
Michel Foucault

IN THE SHADOW
OF THE SILENT MAJORITIES
Jean Baudrillard

69 WAYS TO PLAY THE BLUES
Jürg Laederach

INSIDE & OUT OF BYZANTIUM
Nina Zivancevic

CHAOSOPHY
Félix Guattari

MICROPOLITICS OF DESIRE
Félix Guattari

CHAOS & COMPLEXITY
Félix Guattari

▲ AUTONOMEDIA NEW AUTONOMY SERIES ▲
JIM FLEMING & PETER LAMBORN WILSON, EDITORS

FRIENDLY FIRE
Bob Black

CALIBAN AND THE WITCHES
Silvia Federici

X TEXTS
Derek Pell

TAZ
TEMPORARY AUTONOMOUS ZONE,
ONTOLOGICAL ANARCHY,
POETIC TERRORISM
Hakim Bey

THIS IS YOUR FINAL WARNING!
Thom Metzger

FIRST AND LAST EMPERORS:
THE ABSOLUTE STATE
& THE BODY OF THE DESPOT
Kenneth Dean & Brian Massumi

CRACKING THE MOVEMENT
SQUATTING BEYOND THE MEDIA
Foundation for the Advancement
of Illegal Knowledge

WARCRAFT
Jonathan Leake

THIS WORLD WE MUST LEAVE
AND OTHER ESSAYS
Jacques Camatte

SPECTACULAR TIMES
Larry Law

FUTURE PRIMITIVE
John Zerzan

WIGGLING WISHBONE
STORIES OF PATASEXUAL SPECULATION
Bart Plantenga

INVISIBLE GOVERNANCE
ART OF AFRICAN MICROPOLITICS
David Hecht & Maliqalim Simone

THE ELECTRONIC DISTURBANCE
Critical Art Ensemble

THE LIZARD CLUB
Steve Abbott

WHORE CARNIVAL
Shannon Bell, ed.

CRIMES OF CULTURE
Richard Kostelanetz

CAPITAL AND COMMUNITY
Jacques Camatte

THE ROOT IS MAN
Dwight Macdonald

PIRATE UTOPIAS
MOORISH CORSAIRS
& EUROPEAN RENEGADOES
Peter Lamborn Wilson

▲ SEMIOTEXT(E) NATIVE AGENTS SERIES ▲
CHRIS KRAUS, EDITOR

IF YOU'RE A GIRL
Ann Rower

NOT ME
Eileen Myles

WALKING THROUGH CLEAR WATER
Cookie Mueller

HANNIBAL LECTER, MY FATHER
Kathy Acker

SICK BURN CUT
Deran Ludd

MADAME REALISM COMPLEX
Lynne Tillman

THE NEW FUCK YOU
ADVENTURES IN LESBIAN READING
Eileen Myles & Liz Kotz, eds.

HOW I BECAME ONE OF THE
INVISIBLE
David Rattray

THE ORIGIN OF *THE* SPECIES
Barbara Barg

THE CUTMOUTH LADY
Romy Ashby

READING BROOKE SHIELDS
THE GARDEN OF FAILURE
Eldon Garnet

▲ AUTONOMEDIA BOOK SERIES ▲

SOUNDING OFF!
MUSIC AS SUBVERSION/
RESISTANCE/REVOLUTION
Ron Sakolsky & Fred Wei-Han Ho

UNBEARABLES
The Unbearables

THE DAUGHTER
Roberta Allen

MAGPIE REVERIES
James Koehnline

FILE UNDER POPULAR
THEORETICAL & CRITICAL
WRITINGS ON MUSIC
Chris Cutler

ON ANARCHY &
SCHIZOANALYSIS
Rolando Perez

GOD & PLASTIC SURGERY
MARX, NIETZSCHE,
FREUD & THE OBVIOUS
Jeremy Barris

MARX BEYOND MARX
LESSONS ON THE GRÜNDRISSE
Antonio Negri

RETHINKING MARXISM
Steve Resnick & Rick Wolff, eds.

THE TOUCH
Michael Brownstein

GULLIVER
Michael Ryan

MODEL CHILDREN
Paul Thorez

SCANDAL
ESSAYS IN ISLAMIC HERESY
Peter Lamborn Wilson

THE ARCANE OF REPRODUCTION
HOUSEWORK, PROSTITUTION,
LABOR & CAPITAL
Leopoldina Fortunati

CLIPPED COINS, ABUSED
WORDS, CIVIL GOVERNMENT
Constantine George Caffentzis

TROTSKYISM AND MAOISM
A. Belden Fields

FILM & POLITICS
IN THE THIRD WORLD
John Downing, ed.

COLUMBUS & OTHER CANNIBALS
WÉTIKO DISEASE & THE WHITE MAN
Jack Forbes

THE NEW ENCLOSURES
Midnight Notes Collective

ENRAGÉS & SITUATIONISTS IN
THE OCCUPATION MOVEMENT,
MAY '68
René Viénet

CASSETTE MYTHOS
THE NEW MUSIC UNDERGROUND
Robin James, ed.

XEROX PIRATES
"HIGH" TECH & THE NEW
COLLAGE UNDERGROUND
Autonomedia Collective, eds.

THE NARRATIVE BODY
Eldon Garnet

POPULAR REALITY
Irreverend David Crowbar, ed.

ZEROWORK
THE ANTI-WORK ANTHOLOGY
Bob Black & Tad Kepley, eds.

MIDNIGHT OIL
WORK, ENERGY, WAR, 1973–1992
Midnight Notes Collective

A DAY IN THE LIFE
TALES FROM THE LOWER EAST SIDE
Alan Moore & Josh Gosniak, eds.

GONE TO CROATAN
ORIGINS OF NORTH AMERICAN
DROPOUT CULTURE
J. Koehnline & R. Sakolsky, eds.

ABOUT FACE
RACE IN POSTMODERN AMERICA
Timothy Maliqalim Simone

HORSEXE
ESSAY ON TRANSSEXUALITY
Catherine Millot

DEMONO
(THE BOXED GAME)
P.M.

FORMAT AND ANXIETY
COLLECTED ESSAYS ON THE MEDIA
Paul Goodman

THE DAMNED UNIVERSE
OF CHARLES FORT
Louis Kaplan, ed.

BY ANY MEANS NECESSARY
OUTLAW MANIFESTOS
& EPHEMERA 1965–70
P. Stansill & D. Z. Mairowitz, eds.

THE OFFICIAL KGB HANDBOOK
USSR Committee for State Security

WILD CHILDREN
D. Mandl & P. L. Wilson., eds.